P9-EDM-255

CONTENTS

I Hate Other People's Kids

By Adrianne Frost

Illustrated by Wilson Swain

SIMON SPOTLIGHT ENTERTAINMENT
New York   London   Toronto   Sydney

SIMON SPOTLIGHT ENTERTAINMENT

An imprint of Simon & Schuster

1230 Avenue of the Americas, New York, New York 10020

Text copyright © 2006 by Adrianne Frost

Illustrations copyright © 2006 by Wilson Swain

Manufactured in the United States of America

First Edition 10 9 8 7 6 5 4 3 2 1

Library of Congress Cataloging-in-Publication Data

Frost, Adrianne.

I hate other people's kids / by Adrianne Frost.—1st ed.

p. cm.

ISBN-13: 978-1-4169-0988-0

ISBN-10: 1-4169-0988-5

1. Children—Humor. I. Title.

PN6231.C32F76 2006

818'.602—dc22

2005017610

For my loving husband, Asaf. And my two cats,
who are not children.

ACKNOWLEDGMENTS

I am eternally grateful to the following folks for their assistance and support: my editor, Patrick Price; my cover and interior designer, Sammy Yuen Jr.; Wilson Swain, genius illustrator; the guys and gals at *Best Week Ever*; Annette and Mary at Artists Entertainment Agency; Penny Luedtke and The Luedtke Agency; Karen Herr, Ben Hersey, Brett Ardoin, and Ronney Asher, who are the best friends in the universe; and anyone else I am forgetting. Most importantly, I thank my family (Mom and Luther) for their undying belief in my abilities.

SECTION FOUR: *How to Deal*

Introduction

I hate Other People's Kids. I hate them with a vengeance.

I don't like to see them, smell them, or hear them. I find that most of the precious little tots I come into contact with start out cute but undoubtedly evolve into tornadoes of screaming and kicking. Kids are a chaotic mess of drool and squeaks, and I hereby give you license to hate them too.

Oh, the blasphemy! "You're not supposed to hate kids!" "They're adorable!" "What is wrong with you?" These are probably a fraction of some of the things you've heard if you've said you don't care for children. Along with disparaging comments, you get rolling eyes, clutched-at chests, and parents who cover their kids' ears and hustle the tots away as if you're about to devour them. Well, fear not, dear reader, for you are not alone.

All of us, with or without children, have had that sinking feeling come over us when we see kids sitting in a movie theater, because we know there will be noise and popcorn thrown and that *smell*, that strange child-smell that follows them around. We've felt nauseous and angry when being seated next to a family of six at our favorite eatery. The dinner has already been disrupted by a soggy cracker that you have to wipe off your seat, hurled with glee from a nearby highchair. And who hasn't gone shopping and turned down an aisle that looks like monkeys attacked it, only to realize it was a group of ten-year-old boys?

There are some people who will say, "Why don't you just hate old people? They're pretty cantankerous." I'll tell you why: Old people have *earned* the right to be pissy. Kids haven't. Kids have everything handed to them even before they're born. They spend nine months in warm, gelatinous goo, eating what Mommy eats and posing for ultrasound pictures like embryonic supermodels. They come into the world as little angels, screeching and flailing. Then they're bathed, fed, wiped, and doted on until they're in their early to late teens, and they milk it every step of the way as if they deserve it all.

Adrianne Frost

The unending permissiveness and passiveness with which parents treat their kids ends up dampening your enjoyment of everyday life. Often a child's tantrum in a public place is met with a soft pat on the bottom and an unapologetic smile at the poor souls who had to witness and hear it. Bawling children are left to "cry it out," without acknowledgment from the parents, while we have to listen to them stammer and spit until they're hoarse. For God's sake, give the kid a cookie and shut him up!

Well, praise the Lord and pass the ammo, because I'm here to say that you don't have to feel guilty about hating Other People's Kids. Yes, kids look like little cherubs when they're sleeping. Yes, you may even have little loved ones yourself. Yes, they seem like manna from heaven. But you don't have to like *every* kid you come into contact with. Other People's Kids yell, scream, cry, plot, steal, trick, annoy, destroy, and do all sorts of other things to make you hate them. In fact, it's perfectly acceptable to out-and-out dislike them before they do anything at all. We have rights too! We have the right not to get screamed at, stepped on, or kicked by kids. We have the right to openly snicker at other people's spawn as they're dragged out of the Toys "R" Us, or to glare at people when they're changing poopy diapers in the middle of Pizza Hut.

There are so many kids to hate, so little time. They've grown in number and type. There are smart-ass kids, wholesome kids, genius kids, scary kids, and the kids that you can't quite put a finger on, but you know you hate them. And there are so many reasons to hate kids. They turn your public and private time into a circus; they can spoil the most peaceful locale. They're not always infants, not always toddlers, not always tweens . . . but they're always annoying.

I have often thought of printing up T-shirts that read I H8 YR KID, just to put it out there. Let's finally release the secrecy and start the hating. There's no shame in it and no need to be afraid. We've hidden our anger for too long, suffering through our share of intolerable baby showers and school plays. It's our turn now. Prepare to be liberated.

Adrianne Frost

A Brief History of Hating Other People's Children

Hating Other People's Kids didn't start with our generation. Are you kidding me? It goes *way* back. Here's a historical perspective:

- During the prehistoric days, at the dawn of man, there was probably a kid crying while others were trying to look at cave paintings.
- Later, the Romans forbade children at orgies, but there was always someone there who couldn't get a sitter.
- They say Jesus loved the little children—all the children of the world—but he never had to dine with one. He chose the lepers.

- George Washington is sworn into office as the first president of the United States on April 30, 1789. His son climbs onto the podium and makes fart noises, so Washington cuts short his inaugural speech, excusing his son for being "tired."
- In 1888 George Eastman invents the Kodak camera, thereafter forcing friends to look at sepia-toned copies of other people's children over and over again.
- In 1908 Henry Ford develops the first automobile. Daughter, Sally Ford, develops the phrase, "Are we there yet?"
- In 1938 *Snow White and the Seven Dwarfs* is Walt Disney's first full-length animated film, opening the floodgates for children's need to see the same movie forty-five times. And to quote it incessantly.
- In the 1940s there is a baby boom—a million babies are born. The birthrate exceeds 20 percent. The little buggers are everywhere.
- During the 1950s television introduces fictional characters of annoying children: Eddie Haskell, Dennis the Menace, the Beaver's friend Lumpy. The world begins to realize kids aren't all that precious.
- In 1976 Ted Turner establishes WTBS Superstation in

Adrianne Frost

Atlanta, Georgia, which shows cartoons in the afternoon. The country finds a new babysitter: TV.

- In the 1980s children become a demographic. In 1983 bloodthirsty parents frantically try to buy Cabbage Patch Dolls for their kids. Many lives are lost.
- A sheep is cloned in 1997, putting the fear of God into people who hate children.
- The new millennium arrives. Ten-year-old girls dress like Britney Spears and boys wear their big jeans pooling around their ankles, talking about getting their freak on. "Pardon/Excuse me," "I'm sorry," and "May I," fall out of the vernacular.
- In 2006 *I Hate Other People's Kids* becomes a revelation for all people who have been afraid to admit their hatred. A revolution begins!

Quiz: You Down with Other People's Kids (OPK)?

1. **The last movie you saw was:**
    a. a videotape of Arcadia Elementary's *Three Billy Goats Gruff* performance.
    b. some Jim Carrey movie.
    c. *Debbie Does Dallas*.

2. **The placenta is:**

   a. a by-product of birth.

   b. a slimy, magenta goo.

   c. a wonderful appetizer.

3. **Your friend can't get a sitter for your birthday celebration. You:**

   a. tell her to bring her baby to the party.

   b. offer to help her find someone to babysit.

   c. wish her well and drink until you don't know your name.

4. **An eight-year-old is making loud noises on the bus. Do you:**

   a. ask him to stop.

   b. ask his parents to tell him to stop.

   c. tell him Santa will die if he doesn't shut up.

5. **Children are to movie theaters as fish are to:**

   a. aquariums.

   b. bowls.

   c. movie theaters.

Adrianne Frost

6. **During a romantic dinner in a restaurant, a little girl throws mashed potatoes in your hair. You:**

   a. laugh, then wipe it out of your hair with a napkin.

   b. cry, then wash it out in the bathroom.

   c. scream and throw your salmon at her head.

7. **Your best friend asks you to be her son's godmother/father. You tell her:**

   a. you don't know if you can handle the responsibility.

   b. you are already booked up.

   c. only if you have the power to turn off life support.

8. **A little girl in a store asks if you've seen her mommy. You:**

   a. rush her to the security guard.

   b. use your cell phone to call 9-1-1.

   c. begin signing frantically and speaking like Marlee Matlin.

9. **True or false: A child just kicked you.**

   a. True

   b. False

   c. Yes, but I kicked back.

10. Finish this quote: "Spare the rod, spoil _____"

    a. the child.

    b. the Earth.

    c. *me*.

Scoring

Mostly *a*s: You should tattoo "Welcome" on your forehead. You are way too down with OPK.

Mostly *b*s: You try your best to lie and cheat your way out of it, but you still get suckered in by the parents and the kids. Moderately down.

Mostly *c*s: Congratulations! You are *definitely* not down with OPK. You don't take shit from anyone, regardless of their size. Remind me not to piss you off.

Identifying the Enemy

"CHILDREN ARE ALL FOREIGNERS."
—RALPH WALDO EMERSON

Before you can conquer your enemy or, in this case, another person's obnoxious child, you must discover as much as you can about their characteristics. If you have the foresight and are hypervigilant, you can recognize these kids and get out of their path.

The Hellbound Tyke

These are kids who are easy to spot and avoid. They're the ones who wear their dysfunction like badges at a convention for the irritating: "Hi, my name is Tyrant!" Like most genera of animals in the wild, there are subspecies of the Hellbound Tyke. Should you find yourself in the vicinity of the Hellbound Tyke, run—you can still make it out alive. You stand a chance if you know the signs and can plan your escape route early.

Little Monsters

The first type of Little Monster is the NINJA. These kids are deceptively calm on the surface. But think twice before being fooled by the pressed Gap Kids outfit, the *Weekly Reader* magazine (or Little Golden Books) tucked under the arm, and the clincher: two front teeth missing from their adorable little smile. Precious, right? *Ha!* The second the parent's back is turned, they kick their siblings. They pull their dogs' ears. They bite their playmates. They build neutron bombs. Then, right as you're about to say something to their parents about the kid's behavior, they sprout angel wings and a halo and go back to reading *The Pokey Little Puppy* with wide eyes. From the safety of their book, they make eye contact with you and give you that look. You know the one, the "What are you going to do about it? Tell on me? They'll never believe you!" look. All you can do is gnash your teeth and ball up your fists, because they're right, damn it! If only everyone was given a camera phone in order to record the devious antics of Other People's Children. Maybe then we'd have some justice. It would be like *Cops* for the under-twelve set: "*Kids,* filmed in Terrorvision." Until then, make sure to wear your running shoes to the mall.

The second type of Little Monster is the TASMANIAN DEVIL, the child who runs rampant, leaving havoc and destruction in his or her wake. You can hear their screaming and hollering, like banshees, from the next shopping aisle. Accompanying their vocals is the sound of inventory slamming to the ground, courtesy of outstretched arms continually whirling like an uncontrollable windmill. Even Don

Quixote wouldn't joust with these kids. They aren't angry or upset over anything; they just love to demolish everything in their path. The annihilation of something—*anything*—is their goal. Whether it's a stack of toilet paper or a pyramid of acrylic tumblers, it's oh so much fun to watch them fall down! And you're forced to gingerly step around the carnage as a weeping store clerk comes around to clean it all up for the third time in a single shift (at minimum wage).

Finally beware of the LINEBACKER, the child bearing huskiness. These aren't the fat kids (we'll get to them later); these are unusually large and hormonally charged kids who pick on everyone else. Georgy Porgy "kissed the girls and made them cry," right? What no one ever talks about is that Georgy weighed one hundred and forty pounds and wore an adult-size extra-large T-shirt. *That's* why the girls cried; he sat on them and forced a kiss on them. It was sexual harassment for second graders. Big kids look at you like you're a challenge to beat up, push down, and gobble. It makes you wonder if Doritos have enhancing drugs in them: "Cool Ranch, now with more 'roids!" These genetic giants know they have the power to kick anyone's ass, especially adults. All grown-ups placate big kids to save having their asses handed to them by a ten-year-old.

> **Examples:** The Bad Seed, Damien, Cousin Oliver from *The Brady Bunch*, Tabitha from *Bewitched*, Angelica from *Rugrats*, that kid from *Problem Child*, Kevin from *Home Alone*, Dennis the Menace, Nelson Muntz, Eddie Haskell, and Bamm-Bamm Rubble.

Agitators

Some people think it's clever when kids have smart mouths. It's like when owners define their dog's tricks and mood swings as, "She thinks she's people!" except with kids, it's, "She thinks she's a grown-up!" And they're treated the same way as dogs, as if it's the most amazing thing ever! This child is the SECOND-RATE COMEDIAN. The act is not cute. It's annoying. It's insolence. Once kids think that cursing, being sarcastic, or correcting a grown-up is acceptable, forget it. They'll spout damns and hells with a self-satisfied smirk as the room erupts into laughter and their parents feign shock. You've got a little Lenny Bruce running its mouth and reveling in adult's responses. "Thank you, I'm here all night. Try the veal!"

ENCYCLOPEDIA BROWNS are those kids who voraciously watch the Discovery and History channels, and The

Learning Channel, and then pass every tidbit they've absorbed onto you. Let's say, for instance, you mention that you are interested in adopting a cat. This six-year-old Poindexter will start in about the history, timeline, and recorded tales of every cat that has ever lived. I'm not talking just housecats. This kid will finish with the domesticated breeds, and then immediately launch into the big cats: tigers, lions, snow leopards. *Snow leopards?* What the hell? You just want to rescue a tabby.

Sometimes you find yourself in the grip of the tyke who doesn't shut up: the RAMBLER. They talk continuously, and they don't have the ability to segue. For example, they went to the playground, and they swung on the swings, and they ate a hot dog, and the sky is blue today, and cats don't like water, and baby frogs are called "tadpoles." Listening to them feels like some perverted hypnosis. Your eyelids keep getting heavy, but you can still hear them. The other type of motormouths are the kids who have no internal censor whatsoever. Not only do they ask inappropriate questions, they give out way too much information: "Why is that man faaaaaaaat?" "My daddy sleeps on the couch." "My mommy's ka-gina is itchy."

Examples: The chicken hawk that Foghorn Leghorn babysits, the Bad News Bears, Bart Simpson, Russell from *Fat Albert*, the kid from *Jerry Maguire*, Chicken Little, Milhouse Van Houten, and Scrappy-Doo.

For Your Consideration: Ugly Babies

A lot of people will reason, "Sure, I hate Other People's Kids, but no one could hate a baby." To these people, I present Ugly Babies. Why hate them? Well, first off, they're ugly. We're not talking cute-ugly, like Mickey Rooney. I speak of the baby that, if you put a cigar in its mouth, would seriously resemble that bald-headed guy from *The Shield*. This is the kind of ugly that you've woken up with after a heavy night of tequila body shots. You shrink away from Ugly Babies and try to conceal your horror from the unknowing parents. And it's not just infants. Some toddlers are hideous, hideous creatures. Their heads are *huge*; disturbingly too big for their bodies. And they're forever in coveralls stained with spittle.

Even when Cute Babies cry, they turn ugly. But when an Ugly Baby cries, it's like Mars collapsing in on itself—just red and mush. Ugly Toddlers look like mummified Oompa-Loompas, or like the sunburned elderly when they cry. Their faces turn from crimson to magenta. Their sausage arms flap like pigs ready for takeoff. Sounds similar to the ones heard in *The Exorcist* bubble out with drool.

And finally take note of this: Ugly Babies' poop is especially potent. Perhaps it is their anger escaping, but they always seem to poop when they enter your personal space. And the smell lingers after they're gone, like an unspoken evil.

They're Just Asking for You to Hate Them

Maybe you hate these kids (maybe you were *like* these kids), but some children are just looking to get their asses kicked. No one on God's green earth should have a fanny pack, pocket protector, or walk with waistlines that reach their armpits (add ten hate points if they carry a knapsack). These children also have a wealth of knowledge about inane subjects (like dung beetles). While most kids are tearing it up on the playground, these guys are drooling over logarithms and cosigns. There's nothing wrong with being smart. There *is* something wrong with a second grader dressing like an insurance adjuster and having "Gandalf rules!" written on their notebook.

One of the most universally hated type of kid is the OBNOXIOUS FAT KID. You see them everywhere, whining and pining for a bag of Funyuns. It's so obvious that these giant Weebles are overfed and underdisciplined. It's not their fault that they're fat. It is, however, their fault that they become loud and angry when they don't get their way. It's easy to understand that they are used to pitching fits and being placated with food. Nonetheless, it's not easy to forgive their meaty little sausage feet stepping on your Manolo Blahniks as they have a stomping tantrum when their mothers refuse to buy the six-pack of Snickers. I mean, who didn't cheer a little when Augustus Gloop fell into Willy Wonka's chocolate river?

Another type you instinctively hate is the HOOKER/ PIMP kid. Come on, there isn't at least one of us who hasn't been shocked by a kid who's dressed too old for his or her age. Granted, a lot of kids want to be grown-up, but it's really disgusting to see a girl wearing hipsters and a belly-baring T-shirt. Add sparkly, fake tattoos and pierced ears, and you've got yourself a hoochie mama. And speaking of dressing up a child like a thirty-year-old Texas real-estate agent, baby beauty pageants are just a travesty. Little girls prance around, like when Janet Jackson did her Cher impression with a boa on *Good Times*, dancing and shaking like they're about to do a pole dance. The worst thing is, they grow little egos in their little heads and are suddenly "princesses" (meaning, spoiled). Little boys shouldn't dress like gangstas and pimps, either. When did Garanimals start making giant, baggy jeans and Michael Jordan Ts? What do you do, match gat to gat? Shame on you, Baby Phat!

Examples: Urkel, Screech, Spanky, the Beav's Lumpy, Eric Cartman, Piggy from *Lord of the Flies*, Lolita, Chachi, Jodie Foster in *Taxi Driver*, Jodi Foster in *Bugsy Malone*, and Jodie Foster in *Foxes*.

Whether it's furrowing their brow or ordering crème brûlée instead of a sundae, kids who act grown-up are just plain creepy. Parents love when their kids make adult expressions (meaning, looking stressed or ponderous). If a child is making those faces, he's in need of a Xanax, not encouragement. The kid doesn't want giggles; he requires therapy.

Little boys who like to wear three-piece suits, even to school and soccer practice, aren't adorable. They've been possessed by the ghost of a Wall Street broker. And little girls who want to wear heels and get manicures are taking the train to Implant Land later in life. If you want them to be more mature, let them take jobs. Reenact child-labor laws. We've gotten rid of the coal mines, so there's really no danger to them. It will teach them responsibility, and they won't look so out of place in those outfits.

The Hidden Menace

These children unsuspectingly swoop in on you. They look normal. They're even cute. But they wear their dysfunction on the inside. Just when you think they're okay, they'll eat their boogers, cry at the drop of a hat, or urinate in your lap while grinning broadly.

Disconcerting Children

KIDS WHO WON'T TALK TO YOU: It's beyond shyness; it's weirdness. When you ask a question, they whisper the answer into their parent's ears. The kid hides behind his parent's legs, like a little Maltese who only responds to treats. You take your dog to the park to encourage socialization with other dogs, don't you? So the kid needs to be pushed out there to learn to run with the pack. I'm not equating children with dogs, but . . . okay, I'm equating children with dogs. The most annoying thing is that these small mimes are a vast waste of your time. In the hours it takes to coax them out of their shell, you could've had coffee with a friend, gone to see a movie, and stood in line at the bank (all vastly more rewarding).

KIDS WHO, WITH NO ENCOURAGEMENT, BOND TO YOU LIKE A PARASITE: They are rubber and you are glue, and they'll never leave you alone. Probably it's because you're the coolest one in the room, or, no doubt, you're infinitely cooler than their parents. Like little bathroom attendants, they're always waiting outside the loo when you're done. If you're flirting with a hot prospect, there they are, asking if you'll get them a juice. When you're ready to go, you find them hiding in your coat, trying to hitch a ride. And suddenly herpes isn't looking so bad after all. It seems better to have a blister on your privates for the rest of your life than a child latching on to you at a party. At least there's a cream for herpes.

CREEPY KIDS: How to explain it? They give you the willies, anxieties, and chills. You know the ones. They stare a lot. You're having a perfectly good conversation with someone, and then the hairs on the back of your neck stand up. You turn around and those big, hollow, Margaret Keane eyes are gaping at you. They speak in different voices, usually to embody their invisible friend (in movies, it's the one that kills people). Their science projects involve death, dying, or disease ("Timmy did a project on how blood clots"). They see dead people. Their last name is sometimes Culkin.

THE NEVER FRIENDLESS: These children carry "friends" with them wherever they go. It can be a "wubbie," a Cabbage Patch Kid, hell, even a turnip with google eyes glued to it. It's a little odd to carry around a security item once they're older than six. The worst part is when they drop or lose the "friend," or if someone tries to take it away. You would think someone chopped off their leg and cauterized it with a Bunsen burner. The shattering cries are like those of soldiers in the Civil War, biting those bullets and gulping whiskey as the amputations began.

This phenomenon has been made far worse with the introduction of the American Girl dolls. If you haven't seen them, they are multi-ethnic and are often bought to resemble the child who holds them. The child and doll can have matching outfits, too. Should the mother have a similar ensemble too, the three of them look like Russian nesting dolls.

Examples: Wednesday Addams, Pebbles Flintstone, Sally Brown (Charlie's sister), Danny Torrance, Regan McNeill, the kids from *The Ring* and *The Sixth Sense*, and Harry Potter.

Adrianne Frost

Parents Think It's Cute but It Isn't: Dressing Up Kids Like Dolls

I am ashamed to admit it, but one of the funniest things I ever saw was a pug dressed in a bomber jacket. A dog doesn't have free will, and apparently neither do some kids until they're twelve. How else can you explain babies and toddlers in ridiculous clothing and accessories? It's as if people had children just so they could dress them up. Themed outfits especially are a travesty. A child should never be clad in a princess or cowboy outfit as everyday wear. But you see it all the time. Kids already live in a fantasy world; now they're dressed for it. If they weren't already getting picked on at school, you can count on it now.

Infants suffer the most. They truly have no say in what goes on their bodies. If you hear a blood-curdling scream at the local mall, it's usually because a six-month-old baby is having its ears pierced (it won't be so cute when the kid's fourteen and has keloids and cauliflower ear). Parents everywhere routinely dress their babies like flappers, with silly lace headbands around their noggins. Add the earrings and a newborn girl looks like a saloon whore. (And P.S., a baby does not need a bow in its three hairs.)

You want to dress up your kids? Put your boy in coveralls to become Painter Man. Have him tackle the spare room. Bedeck your daughter in a maid's outfit; she can come over and clean my house. Or create a spa with the littlest masseuses. The world will thank you.

What the Hell Is Wrong with This Kid?

You've gotta laugh uncomfortably at kids who continually swipe at their ears, when there's not a fly in sight. Stranger still are the ones whose eating habits are bizarre. While other children want Rooty Tooty Fresh and Fruity at the IHOP, they order chicken marsala and clap their hands when it appears before them. And a lot of kids eat dirt, but there are those who create entire buffets out of the stuff. There's something not quite right about these children. And, yet, the tests come back fine. . . .

DRAMA QUEENS: These kids have been taking acting, singing, and dancing lessons since they were in the womb.

AND—EVERYTHING—THEY—SAY— IS—VERY—AN—NI—MA—TED!!

They insist on going to band or theater camp, declaring their imminent suicide should they be denied. They get up at parties and sing all verses and choruses of "You Light Up My Life," demanding silence and everyone's full attention. During their Christmas vacation, they memorize the entire four-hour lyrics of the *Les Misérables* CD, or study piano until their fingers bleed, because they're gonna "make it," goddamn it!

CHILDREN WHO TURN STATEMENTS INTO QUESTIONS: "Did you know that I can say 'sneeze' while I sneeze?" "Did you know I have to go to the bathroom?" "Can I want French fries?" "Why do you have that mole? Why don't you get it removed? Do you want cancer?" "Don't I like birds?" They speak to you like you're the Magic 8-Ball. All signs point to NO.

THE CHILD WHO STINKS: Does no one but you smell this kid? He reeks of Cheese Nips and feet. Jesus! Huggies should create a kiddie body spray and promote hygiene like they do with Pull-Ups: "I'm a clean kid now." When you're around a malodorous toddler, don't pull punches. Don't ask "What's that smell?" in your most polite voice, avoiding eye contact with the parent. Turn to the mother or father of the offending child and state, "For God's sake, your kid stinks! Dip him into a bath at once! Hose him down. He's fungal!" Someone has to do it.

Examples: Ralph Wiggum, Bobby Brady, DJ from *Roseanne*, Baby June, Margaret O'Brien, Danny Partridge, Olivia from *The Cosby Show*, Zuzu, and Pigpen.

So Good It Hurts (Saints, Cripples, and Child Stars)

Sugary sweet and perfect in every way, you can't find a flaw with these children. That's why you hate them. Kids with cancer that create their own foundations, that neighborhood boy who donated his eyes. The kid who lost his puppy to anal polyps and created a telethon for the disease. If they're so great at that age, what does that say about you now? You, who never volunteer, give to charity, or open the door for old people. These saccharine children are dirty mirrors that make you reexamine your own life. No thank you.

Adrianne Frost

OVERACHEIVERS: The little girl who was nominated for an Oscar at ten. And won. She goes on *The Tonight Show with Jay Leno* and gets asked all kinds of inane questions like, "So, do you have a boyfriend?" as the audience goes "Awwwww!" No, she doesn't have a boyfriend. She's *ten*! But she bats her eyelashes and says, "Maaaaaybe." Ugh! Then Leno asks, "What do you want to be when you grow up?", and she'll usually answer "doctor" or "veterinarian." But what she should really say is "heroin addict," because that's the most likely career trajectory for child actors. And who hasn't, at one time or another, wanted to kick the crapola out of the Olsen twins? Not just because they're the friggin' *Olsen twins*, but because they've accomplished more in nineteen years than most of us will in our entire lives.

WE INTERRUPT THIS PROGRAM: Annoying kids on television have grown since the Bradys. This goes way beyond Punky Brewster territory. Sure, sitcom kids are annoying as hell, but the ones in commercials are just as bad, if not worse, because they appear uninvited. They force their siblings to eat food that is questionable ("He likes it, hey, Mikey!"); they stuff their pants full of Charmin to land softly on their butts as they roller skate in the house; they exhaust the supply of Bounty towels, because they wanted to pour their own juice (recycling, anyone?). Even worse are the kids exploited on live morning shows and for what? So the world can see evil spawn, red faced and bawling, on national television? Their parents holding them up like beacons for Al Roker. The tots then slobber on the mike, talk in gibberish, or hide their faces. How adorable! I just want my friggin' weather report.

Examples: Shirley Temple, Anne Frank, Corky in *Life Goes On*, Dakota Fanning, Ricky Schroeder from *The Champ*, "L'il Inventors" from Letterman, that four-year-old who knows all about presidents, Mary-Kate and Ashley, Punky Brewster, and Mikey.

!Tales from the Front Line!

My eighteen-month-old niece *proclaimed*—*very* loudly—"I pooped!! I pooped!!" during both my grandmother's funeral and my wedding. Luckily, during my wedding, I was convinced she was saying, "I do." —Lawcomic

Adrianne Frost

SECTION TWO

Public Places

"THE TROUBLE WITH CHILDREN IS THAT
THEY ARE NOT RETURNABLE."
—QUENTIN CRISP

Now that we've identified the types of children we can't stand, let's look at their particular behaviors that make us crazy. This section exposes why we hate Other People's Kids in public places. There are so many things OPK do in public that are infuriating, so many places they shouldn't be allowed, so many actions that make us grateful for birth control.

Shopping

Many of us live to shop. The exhilaration of finding the perfect bargain surpasses even the most intense orgasm. (And it lasts longer.) When we can't afford a vacation, we can still afford to buy ourselves a little something nice! Sometimes just browsing can put us into a state of Zen. The experience of shopping is an absolute miracle.

That is, until the presence of children wreaks havoc upon the shopping experience, and your beloved Zen is torn to shreds like confetti. Because of kids, we shoppers have had to evolve into soldiers, fearing and contemplating the next guerilla attack in the sporting goods department, painting on camouflage before even going near the Sears Portrait Studio.

Crouching Parent, Hidden Monster

For a night on the town, people with kids get a babysitter. Why no one thinks to get a sitter to go shopping is beyond me. Instead the entire family piles into the SUV and makes that communal trek to a superstore. Upon arrival they appear to endlessly climb out of the gas-guzzling vehicle as if it is a clown car, stack two children on top of each other in the store's cart and make the other two hold on to each side. There's always a big "Ohp-pah!" when they finally get into their configuration, looking like one of those Chinese balancing acts from Cirque du Soleil. Then the parents make their kids promise to stay *right where they are,* walking alongside the basket, and under no circumstances are they to stray from that position. The little tykes promise to the grave to stay by their parents. Bullshit.

Adrianne Frost

Children get loose, like sailors in Bangkok hungrily looking for whores, and they turn the store into their own private amusement park. I blame Mickey D's. With the creation of the McDonald's Playland, McDonald's revolutionized the idea of combining playtime with dinnertime. Kids had found a place to run and jump alongside the eating area. Unfortunately for us, kids now carry this expectation wherever they go. If they can't get their folks to take them to Playland, then OPK will bring Playland to themselves.

Kids love to chase one another in stores. Shiny, round, silver racks stuffed to the fullest with merchandise offer the perfect setting for this sport. It isn't even a *real* game. There's no consistent course, no one's the hunter, and no one's It. It's just running, running, *running* willy-nilly around the stacks of sweatpants and leggings and, eventually, your legs. Now *you're* part of the obstacle course. You would think that someone, *anyone*, would apologize, at least by the fifth time they run into you. You want to yell, "My knees! I'm not supposed to get kids on them!" as you fall dramatically to the ground. Not that anyone would bother to notice your anguish. The only peace from the jumping, squealing, yelling, and destroying comes when they're ushered into another department, soon to annihilate

Housewares by hitting one another with frying pans, or Women's Hosiery, where they relish putting pantyhose on their heads. In their wake it looks like Hiroshima as shell-shocked workers in red vests and name tags weep while refolding sweaters and the Muzak version of "The End" by the Doors plays mournfully overhead.

Running around isn't the only in-store entertainment for tiny terrors. Kids have an entire Rolodex of destructive games in their brains. There's Brat Racing in the aisles. Each aisle becomes a track for a hyped-up child. You're forced to crane your neck around each corner, as if entering the freeway. Otherwise it's—*Crash! Bang!*—into your cart, and when the drag-racing kid starts crying, you'll be the one blamed for not looking where you were going.

In mega- and superstores, hide-and-seek has become a juvenile art form. Displays are now hiding places. Bins filled with stock are prime spots to take cover—a place for kids to duck behind or get in, then jump out and scream, scaring the bejesus out of their siblings and those shopping in the vicinity. "Surprise! I'm a little asshole!" they may as well yell with a psychotic grin and a thong on their head. It's enough that the elderly or unstable shouldn't attempt to shop on a weekend, unless they have an EMT accompany them.

Adrianne Frost

A rage simmers within you as you navigate aisles strewn with merchandise that some kid threw on the ground, the wheels of your cart catching on a hand towel. And you must sacrifice your last slivers of Zen-like calm so as to not trip a pair of sibling tots running up the down escalator.

What a relief it would be to have a designated area to contain children! Instead of Playland, it would be Stayland. I envision a kiddie corral, surrounded by *mildly* electric fencing in bright yellow and red. The jolts would be just enough to warn them, but not enough to hurt them. Honestly, you have to set boundaries, right? It wouldn't be

a torture chamber. It would even be enjoyable for them. In fact the enclosure would be designed with aisles, shopping carts, boxes, piles of underwear—all the things kids love about playing in stores. Children of all ages would roam, free range, in the roundup, like little calves. If they got too rambunctious, they'd be roped and hog-tied with silly string. How fun! There could even be a sugar-free snack bar in the corral, stocked full of milk and turkey, and little cushioned cots for when the tryptophan kicks in. Providing this service for free would undoubtedly bring in more paying customers with kids. The store would once again be a quiet, safe, and even fun haven. Free margaritas for everyone!

The Sound of Music

When waiting for parents to pick out their purchases, kids get restless or bored, or feel ignored. While Mommy reads for the thread counts at Bed, Bath & Beyond, her little Willy Loman will *not* go unnoticed. Attention must be paid! Little inventive minds find a way to create the most annoying, repetitive noises imaginable. First he kicks his feet vigorously, the thump of his shoes barely registering on the sound scale. This soon gets boring, because no one's paying attention to him. So he takes the first thing he finds that will make some noise, and he begins to clink it against the shopping basket. The *clink* is usually faint, like a hummingbird feeding on nectar. But Mommy's still glued to those sheets. The *clink* grows to a *clank* as the hummingbird grows into a buzzard, circling its prey. People begin to wonder what is that noise. Are the pipes creaking? Is the Tin Man near? Is there a buzzard in the store? This is not enough attention to satisfy the child trapped in the cart, though. So *clank* turns to *bang*. And not just bang, but *BANG! BANG! BANG! BANG! BANG!* The buzzard's now a 747. Heads are turning, people's ears begin to bleed, but this little symphony still isn't enough for him, so he starts singing. What song this is, no one knows, because it is completely made up and has no discernable lyrics. Everyone in the store has tears of pain coming out of their eyes as if the sound system suddenly switched to Yanni.

Just as the manager and a mob of angry patrons with torches come to get this cacophonous echolalia to end, Mommy stands up to attend to her child. He stops making the noise and smiles at everyone smugly as she wheels him over to look at shower curtains. Mission accomplished: Everyone in the store has given him their full interest. Should Mommy turn away too long, however, say, to a duvet that's on sale . . . the vicious cycle will begin again.

Your punishment is that you now have to stay out of the section in which this wunderkind sits, which makes your shopping trip two hours longer than planned.

As a solution clowns should be employed to distract children while their parents shop. It would leave them entertained or terrified, who cares which? Or place small terrariums, filled with box turtles and hermit crabs, throughout the store for the kids to look at while they're being abandoned for oven mitts. Personally I would like to install giant timers onto the children's arms, set for thirty minutes. That would be all the time the parents would be allowed in order to pick up what they need. If they don't meet the deadline, they and their kids are escorted out of the store . . . by clowns.

Gimme, Gimme, Gimme

The "I Want" rant is a precisely choreographed production that we've all witnessed. It is brought on by the fact that shiny, brightly colored toys are purposely kept right at a child's eye level. Somehow those vibrant, pleasurable items hypnotize children into creating the familiar scene. We've all seen it at one time or another. For example, a little girl lifts up an object, just light enough for her to carry, and goes to

　　　　Adrianne Frost

her parents like a reanimated zombie with dead, doll eyes. That child knows that through the right amount of repetitive asking, hysterical screaming, and wide-eyed pleading, she can get her parents to buy it for her. But until then, we have to see and hear the epic saga unfold.

The first act is just a simple statement of fact: "I want this." The toy is never, ever, *ever* something that she needs. It won't help with her math, English, or social skills. It's usually something like Rattlesnake Farmer Elmo or Crackwhore Candi (which is really the same old Candi, but accessorized with a crack pipe). It seems harmless enough and the answer is usually no.

In act two the little girl says, her voice getting slightly higher, "I want this" as if she wasn't heard clearly enough the first time. The plot thickens when she is told to put it back. She doesn't. She *must* have this. She's turned into Gollum. "My preciousssssssssssss Candi. We wantssss it."

There is a brief intermission as her eyes well up with tears.

The final act of this show is an aria of piercing shrieks, stomping feet, and tumult until an exasperated father chucks the toy into the cart and the girl's dead eyes come alive again. The suffering crowd applauds the finish of this terrible and pointless production.

The end.

These bad behaviors are all made worse by those miniature, useless, ridiculous shopping carts with the little flags on top. They're supposed to keep the kids busy, distracted, and quiet. Unfortunately these absurd devices empower kids to believe they will actually get the items they throw into it. While most kids do not have purchasing power, they are now able to fill up their own little shopping baskets with Trix, Keebler goodies, candy, and anything in a squeeze tube. Especially potent are vivid, sugary "extreme" titled foods, which equate eating them with bungee jumping. Parents appreciate these carts for keeping their kids occupied, but then the cart, inevitably, has to be emptied and the children learn the device was a ruse. They don't actually get to keep any of the food they picked. We, the shoppers, get to hear again that wonderful opera of screaming.

Perhaps someone could create a comfortable and sturdy apparatus that allows children to be carried on their parents'

Adrianne Frost

heads, away from the toys and games, like women from African villages do. I would call it the Kiddie Lifter, and it would hook around the parents' waist, similar to those back braces for people with scoliosis. Long bars would jut out of the sides, and then sprout up to hold a plastic seat. Of course a seat belt would be attached for Junior's safety, and the item would come in many sizes for different children. The Lifter would be decorated in fabrics sporting elephants, puppies, kitties, and other jolly animals.

There are alternatives, my friends. I call upon shoppers to rally with me: Blindfolds must be handed to kids at the front doors! The greeter could give them out—blue for boys, pink for girls—along with a lollipop. Children are informed that if they keep the blindfold on the entire time, they get the lollipop. They'll feel like they're earning something. Better yet, a strap-on View-Master could be implemented as a store rule: Every child must wear one. They'll be happily entertained by visions from *Benji* or *The Lion King,* and the only noise will be the clicking of the switcheroo.

A last resort is to have parents get their kids hooked on drugs or alcohol. Now, we're not talking crack or speed; those would pump them up. What's say we just inject them with a low dose of Valium when they get into the cart? Or Xanax. Heroin, anyone? Okay, at least plow them with liquor as long as they're not angry drunks. It's sad to see a wasted moppet swinging a lazy fist at another wasted moppet. And make sure there's a savings account to get them through rehab when they turn thirteen.

Until all children are rounded up like cattle, distracted, or turned into junkies, we have to make do with our own creative solutions. Perhaps earplugs, an iPod, or a hearty round of drinking or prayer in the parking lot will bolster you for the experience. Better yet, shop online.

Parents Think It's Cute, but It Isn't: Kids Dressing in Adult Items from the Store

"Oh, look! Frankie's in drag!" Yes, it's very amusing when a child grabs a shift off the rack at Ann Taylor and puts it on. It is not so funny when the parents and sales people later try to get the item off of him. They creep toward him as if he's a very cute rattlesnake, tentative and amused. Frankie is stubborn but coy as he backs away from them, giggling, smack dab into you. Frankie loves being chased! He laughs and screeches, running around the store, knocking over sweaters and T-shirts until he's caught, bawling and kicking. You put down that trench coat you were eyeing and are forced to leave, lest you rip the dress off him yourself.

Movies and Theaters

It should be a law that no kids less than five feet tall are allowed in movies rated greater than G. Parents complain that it's cheaper to take their kids to the movies than to get a sitter. But that's not the case when one of them ends up in the emergency room once another patron snaps after ninety-plus minutes of listening to kids talk, cry, whine, fart, and pitch a fit.

When the screen shows those little cartoons before the feature that say no smoking, throw out your trash, and please be quiet, there should be an added animation that has an enormous hand covering a kid's big, screaming mouth. If that doesn't drive home the point, create a short film with the classic Universal Studios monsters (Frankenstein's monster, the Wolfman, and the Mummy) eating a disruptive child. We must use whatever means necessary to keep the quiet.

"Mommy, What Are Titties?"

When you stand in the lobby of a movie theater, waiting to order your snacks and soda, there are a hundred kids running around. You begin to pray: "God, if you exist and care about me and the ten dollars and fifty cents I just spent on this ticket, please let these carousing kids have tickets to *Digger the Dog's Journey to Monkeyland*. Amen." Surely they're not there to see your horror movie, right? Right? Wrong. You walk into the theater, and it's filled with families. The Motion Picture Association of America's rating system is apparently moot, because John and Joan Q Public have brought their toddlers to see sex, violence, and mayhem on the big screen. Come on, people. There's a *reason* kids' movies are eighty minutes long! That's all they can tolerate! As a viewer you know it only takes one iota of kiddie verbosity to ruin a movie. Three quarters into the film—just as the climax is about to happen—the screaming, talking, and whining you've been trying to ignore crescendos. They never nap! And you've turned around so often to shush or stare at them

Adrianne Frost

that your neck begins to hurt. It's hard to focus on the big screen when the little scream is filling the auditorium. Your only consolation is the hope for nightmares they may have from monsters, zombies, and full-frontal Kevin Bacon.

Wheeeee!

One large soda into my movie, my bladder is usually at full capacity, so I dash up the aisle to pee, hoping not to miss much of the plot. I pee quickly, sometimes washing my hands, and then I dash down the aisle to get back to my seat as quickly as possible, apologizing profusely to the people in my row and keeping my silhouette hunched. I am civil and polite.

OPK dash up and down the aisles because they have the attention span of a gnat. Halfway through a movie, say, just as the iceberg is hit in *Titanic,* boredom kicks in for the kiddie set. Not to mention the sugary rush from all of their gobbled sour gummy worms. Since there's not a playground in sight, their parents let loose the tyrants. Hey, it gives Mom and Dad a break. They're too preoccupied watching Leo sketch Kate in the nude. The parents are used to this behavior anyway and tune it out as their kids rush back into the row, begging for more money to play the House of the Dead III game in the lobby, stepping on your feet and never once apologizing.

You're too grown-up to throw popcorn at them and saying "shhhh" has no effect. M&M's may cause eye damage when chucked at the little heathens. So for revenge I recommend Skittles. Chuck them in the aisle and watch as their young asses hit the ground like something out of a Three Stooges short. By using a quiet and gentle lob to scatter the Skittles in the proper configuration, there is also less chance of getting caught.

This Is Not a Tearjerker

You're all settled in with your popcorn and Coke, snuggling with your honey bunny, or hanging with your best friend. You've had a hard day and want to blow off some steam with a comedy. You're watching the latest Will Ferrell flick, but it's pretty tough to laugh away your cares with "I wanna gooooooooooo" in the background. Instead of the parent removing his child from the theater, Daddy tries to coddle her, console her, and quiet her because Daddy refuses to leave. He's gotta see how the film ends. Well, here's some news: The kid's not going to stop! The kid needs to be removed! It's a Will Ferrell comedy, for goodness sake! TAKE YOUR KIDS OUT OF THE FRIGGIN' THEATER AND WAIT FOR THE DVD!

Adrianne Frost

Do the Math: Get a Home-Theater System

Okay, so let's say parents go to the movies every weekend. They bring their two kids. They buy sugary treats for the kids and themselves, then they all sit down to ruin your movie.

Now, let's see what would happen if they stayed home during one month's time and reinvested that money into a home-theater system.

Adult Admissions	$84.00
Child Admissions	$36.00
Popcorn	$36.00
Sodas	$38.00
Candy	$28.00
Nachos for All	$25.00
Therapy for Kids After Seeing *The Ring*, *Dawn of the Dead*, or *The Pianist*	$1,200.00
Hospital Bill for Removal of Your Foot from Their Ass	$800.00
TOTAL	$2,247.00

Wow! They just saved $2,247.00 in one month! They could have a decent, high-end home theater system in a place where their kids can run and cry and ask inane questions! *Genius!*

I Finally Got a Ticket to The Producers

Live theater is different from the movies. It's *live*. There's no surround sound, no trailers, no nachos. Before the curtain rises and the magic of live theater begins, people are politely asked to silence their cell phones. They also should be politely asked to silence their children.

Even though *The Lion King* is made for them, kids don't have to act like *they're* in the jungle. If you're paying a hundred dollars for a ticket to a show, you want to look at the stage, not a small head beckoning you from the back of its seat to play peek-a-boo. And if you're in, say, *A Streetcar Named Desire,* there should be no kids in the theater at all. Believe me, Little Jimmy's not going to be so focused on Tennessee Williams's play that after the show he asks his parents what the Napoleonic Code is. Kids should be cultured, sure, but only if they want to be cultured. No one wants to see a kid stuffed into his Sears suit, being forced to see *The Nutcracker,* squirming, whining, and then crying at the sight of the Rat King.

If you're paying an exorbitant amount of money for a theater ticket, part of the ticket price should go to separating you from the children. There should be a kid check next to the coat check. On a revolving rack, in a small dimly lit room

Adrianne Frost

in which Brahms's "Lullaby" plays, each child would be catalogued and the parent would get a claim ticket. Placed in a quilted potato sack, heads peeking out like in one of those annoying Anne Geddes photos, the gentle swinging of the sack on the conveyor rack will keep them lulled and secure while Nathan Lane tickles your funny bone.

Parent's Think It's Cute, but It Isn't: That Kid's Not Wearing Pants!

Some kids run around naked, some with just a diaper sans pants. What parents don't realize, as their eyes follow their child around, pointing with a finger at the sheer hilarity of it all, is this: Kids shit. And when they do, it's worse than seeing a big dog do it, because a big dog sniffs around, and then hunches up. An untrained child gives no warning. *That's why you put pants on them.* It's even worse if there's no diaper, because then all of it just flows freely, like a coin-operated dispenser that shoots out Skittles. A diaper is not enough, because, and I have seen this, the little plops of poop can overflow out of the Huggies and all over the ground. It's gross. You'd like to think they're kind of like monkeys, but they're *not* like monkeys because there are people who keep monkeys as pets, and they *put diapers on them*! If a child is going to run around commando, parents should put them in a cage, give them bananas, and put a big sign up that reads Bottomless Child, so we can know to avoid that particular exhibit.

Adrianne Frost

Public and Private Transportation

People like to read and relax during their commute. It's so nice to delve into a book or magazine, listen to music, or just sit in rare stillness, letting the day wash away. When you feel the kick-kickity-kick of tiny feet or hear two high-pitched voices bickering over a Slim Jim, you might as well be on the front lines during WWII.

The Long and Whining Road

Without fail the Midget Brigade Circus—full of tumblers, jugglers, clowns, and magicians—always boards your bus or subway. You feel the kick-kickity-kick of tiny feet on the back of your seat. You hear the orchestrations of impish squealing and crinkling bags as juice boxes are expertly thrown from a stroller. If there's a bar to be swung from or danced around like a friggin' maypole, they'll find it. (Where is the lion for them to stick their head in?) And then there's the freak-show transformation a child exhibits when a coat is presented as their destination nears. They go from angel to demon possessed by the introduction of a parka, screaming like there are needles within the puffy sleeves. Hulk no like put on coat!

Then there's what I like to call Hell Time, that period

between 2:15 p.m. and 3:00 p.m., when schools let out. Whatever happened to yellow buses? Where's my tax money going to? Why do eleven-year-olds talk so loud? They're standing right next to one another, loaded down with enormous backpacks that whack you in the head, yet they holler like hillbillies calling from porch to porch.

Houston, We Have a Problem

If dogs and cats need to be confined and hidden on airplanes, then so should children. A plane is a small space. OPK have a serious chance of invading your personal space by just *breathing* too loud. There used to be smoking and nonsmoking sections on planes. In lieu of that there should be kids and no-kids sectioning. Like secondhand smoke, the stress from tolerating kids on planes is hazardous to your health.

Waiting for the plane to arrive and then boarding it is another time when kids are a major pain in the ass. You would think the addition of televisions would distract them, but they're always tuned to MSNBC and the sound is kept low. Let's face it: Chris Matthews is no Grover. No kid's gonna watch that. So, to entertain himself, Little Stevie, instead of looking at the schedule like the rest of us or

Adrianne Frost

accepting the first answer that Dad gave, asks over and over again, "When's the plane coming? Dad . . . Dad . . . *Dad!* When's the plane coming?" Kids love questions even if they don't get an answer. Why? Because they want attention. It's not Twenty Questions, it's One Million Questions, and it usually consists of the same questions repeated over and over again. Meanwhile you have only one: "Why won't you shut the fuck up?"

It sounds very *Little House on the Prairie,* but in the olden days, you sometimes brought a pack of cards onto a plane to entertain yourself. You would play gin rummy or solitaire on the little pull-out trays, or you would read or sleep. You know, *quiet* distractions. In this electronic age them newfangled video games are everywhere. It's not annoying for kids to play their Game Boy Advances. Hey, if it shuts them up, I'll supply the games. But aren't there headphones to plug into these things? It's so rude and obnoxious, like *War of the Worlds* is happening right there in the cabin. It's unfathomable that these thoughtless kids can eliminate all of the aliens in the known universe in less than thirty seconds, but they can't turn down the friggin' volume.

While we're talking about unfairness, many of us travel with our pets. For some people their pets are their children (only quieter). It's distressing to have to place them in a carrier and under your seat (or, worse, in the cargo hold). So, why don't you get to put Rover on your lap during the flight? Babies and toddlers get to sit on their parents' laps, drooling and defecating and crying. Parents don't have to stuff their noisy toddler into their laptop case. I know the cargo hold would be cold, but there's plenty of room in the overhead compartment and things only shift slightly during takeoffs and landings.

Adrianne Frost

Who in the hell thought it was a genius concept to create miniluggage for kids? It's not luggage; it's a backpack on wheels. Strap it on their backs! Who are we kidding? It is not adorable for kids to lug this thing around the airport. Most adults can't keep control of their own luggage on wheels. A child trying to do it is more absurd. Homeland Security needs to keep a tab on these things, because it creates treacherous conditions in the terminal. The diminutive rolling baggage haphazardly veers left and right, creating dangerous hurdles for anyone unlucky enough to trail the little bugger. Plus it slows the kid down, which means it slows the family down, which means traffic in the airport slows to a crawl as you listen helplessly to your flight's final boarding call. No time for a Cinnabon now. Parents need to realize that they're creating gridlock mayhem simply because they want their kid to be "responsible." Do you really think Susie feels more like an adult because she's dragging around a vinyl backpack printed with Care Bears, filled with toys

> and the security blanket she outgrew three years ago?
> It's not a rite of passage. It's a pain in my ass.

I Spy a Kid I Hate

Nothing is more horrifying before a road trip than opening the backseat door of your friend's car and discovering a kid in a child seat. The kid looks like he or she is about to be jettisoned into space on *Apollo 13*. One strap goes across the lap, two straps form an X across the chest, five small bungee cords are pulled here and there for safety, and the casing, with more padding than the psych ward at Rikers, shoots up a foot over and around their heads. There is no escape. You're going to have to be next to the little astronaut for the whole ride. And there's never space for you to spread out and chill for the next three hours because the kid's in the middle—always in the middle—reeking of Wheat Thins and pee.

But you are a consummate adult and try to make the best of it—that is until the kid starts kicking and screaming, and you can't push an eject button to fly to sweet freedom. Instead you're asked to dig out the child's bottle or rattle from some quilted, barf-stained bag on the floor. Then it's your task to administer the bottle or shake the rattle as the red-faced brat yowls like a stuck pig.

What's worse than being stuck in the backseat of a car with a kid who's crying and screaming? Being stuck in the car with a kid who's verbally comatose. It's hard to have a conversation with the people in the front seat when you're rolling down the highway. You don't want to scream during the whole ride in order to be understood. So you try to talk to the strapped-in munchkin next to you. You ask about school. No answer. You ask about friends. No answer. You ask about politics. No answer. Turns out she's "shy." Then you're bored. So, start telling her about you! "My father drank a lot." "I like a good spanking." "I have a hard time having an orgasm." You'll be entertained and satisfied knowing that later she'll ask her mommy what all of that meant. Next time ask ahead if the kid is coming on the trip. Or start doing your thumb exercises. It might be less stressful to hitchhike.

I once had a job that made me hate kids. Almost. In a fit of summer-employment desperation, I signed up to be a theater counselor at an exclusive girls' camp in Maine. When I arrived, I was assigned the title of Costume Designer, because I was the only one of the theater folk who knew how to operate a sewing machine.

Sometime during tech week for a production of *Hans Christian Anderson,* as I was fitting the girl who played the prima ballerina with a fur stole, a tiny little chorus girl marched up and demanded my attention. "AMY!" she hollered, her peasant costume balled up in one fist. "I don't like my costume!" I explained to her that we were a little short on peasant costumes, so she couldn't trade it for another color. "NO!" she howled, pointing at the ballerina, "I WANT A MINK COAT LIKE HER!" I tenderly explained that peasants just don't get fur coats—not in *Hans Christian Anderson* and not in real life, either. She yelled at the top of her lungs, "MY FATHER PAYS YOUR

Adrianne Frost

SALARY!" I hunkered down in front of her, my face level with hers, and said very quietly and very slowly, "Then you tell him that I want a raise for putting up with you." —Amy

Rikki Tikki Tavi

Truck stops and rest areas are designed as meeting places to park after a long ride to stretch and eat. For OPK it's like letting wild mongooses out of their cage. Were there cobras to kill, that would be fine and good, but at these spots all that awaits are junk food, toy-grabbing claw machines, and love testers.

So you're walking slowly toward the plaza, hands on your aching lower back and glad to be out of the car after six hours, when a gaggle of OPK whizzees past you in an effort to be first in line at Bob's Big Boy, or shove quarters into a game that promises a poorly made Shrek doll. Sometimes they hang out in the Stop & Shop, throwing stuffed bears wearing T-shirts emblazoned with a state name, while you try to purchase your bottle of water or your cigarettes.

At designated picnic areas there's a lot less fun to be had. Mom and Dad have packed soggy bologna sandwiches and generic juice drinks, so the kids scream and plead for something out of the two dusty and isolated vending machines. After half an hour of assaulting your ears, they are granted some change to buy cans of Coke and tortilla chips, setting off a sugar and riboflavin high.

Kids make their own fun at these quiet highway spots. And the only place that has any remote possibility of creating any sort of enjoyment is, of course, the restroom. To you it's an unpleasant place of necessity, smelling of urine and covered in graffiti. To them it's the perfect spot for a game of I Spy. There you are, straddled over the toilet, or sitting on a three-foot-high tower of toilet paper, tending to your business while trying to keep the broken stall door closed with one foot or hand. Suddenly a giggle catches your attention. They're *peering in at you,* either by pressing their eye

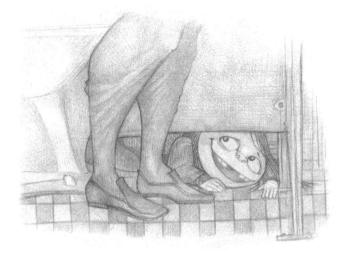

Adrianne Frost

through the stall's gap, or by creeping over the top of the wall while standing on the next-door toilet. You lock eyes with them and they run, squealing, laughing, mocking your pretzel positioning in order to take a pee. You've been duped by a Peeping Tommy.

For Your Consideration: Harnesses and Leashes

In my hippie-dippy college days, I'd float around quoting poetry in my broomstick skirt and loving all living things. I would become very shocked and disgusted with kids who were literally hitched to their parents. "Amnesty for kids!" I would holler. At first glance harnesses and leashes seem very inhumane. At second glance, however, it seems like a bloody good idea. I've switched from the ideals of Save the Children to the NRA. Children who act like animals should be tethered as such. I've seen dogs better behaved than kids, and are far less filthy. Besides, it's awfully funny to see a kid reeled in to his mom like the catch of the day.

Restaurants and Cafés

Families eat out a lot. With more and more family units including two working parents, dining out has become the popular option. It may relieve their stress, but it simultaneously heightens yours. The problem stems from a lack of recognition that different eating establishments cater to different demographics. Should you, for some strange reason, choose to dine at a pizza place with a rat as a mascot, you should expect to see families. But if you go to a fancy eatery with your hard-earned savings to celebrate your anniversary, you don't expect to find a pack of squirming kids there. Extravagant, leisurely dining is not meant for the toddler set. Let them rule the fast food, drive-through sects.

Britney Hates Her Foie Gras

Most upscale establishments do not have a child's menu. Instead they offer nongeneric, unusual, delightful dishes that are meticulously prepared by a chef with an unpronounceable name, who has his own cooking show. You can get pan-seared rosemary salmon or Mediterranean coconut shrimp at a fancy place. At Applebee's, they have chicken quesadillas and cheese fries and sundae supremes made in the kitchen by someone who just got their green card. While you're trying to have a wonderful meal at an upscale restaurant, a mother trying to force-feed Kobe beef to her finicky kid corrupts your dining pleasure. For an hour you have to hear "Eat it. It's just like fried chicken," while the small person cries, "NO." In horror you're forced to watch the mother smother the monk-raised, eighty-dollar slab of beef with ketchup, make the broccoli dance, and resort to threats of no dessert (which is laden with brandy, anyway). "No. *No.* NO!" It's really quite simple: If there are no animated rodents and no ball pit to entertain the children while the greasy pizza pie's in the oven, and the waitstaff is not dressed like barber poles, families need to leave the establishment immediately.

Slip the Maître d' a Fifty

Swanky Joe's is, by nature, a swanky restaurant. You'll pay a ton of money to eat at Swanky Joe's after waiting three months to get a reservation (the proprietor is an Iron Chef). As you triumphantly wait to be seated, you choose to enjoy a cocktail at the bar, which is dipped in gold and was carved in Egypt. It is deeply disconcerting to then have to share this moment of fanciness with a runny-nosed, wheezing small person staring at you. Creepily gazing up at you like an old drunk, she is kicking her little white-stockinged foot against your bar stool while her younger brother makes a game of climbing in and out of the rungs. You are simultaneously revolted and mesmerized by the girl's dried, green torrent of snot, which stretches from nostril to lip bow. And until your name is mercifully called, she catatonically continues to kick your chair and ogle you with her glazed, rheumy eyes. Meanwhile her parents are blissfully laughing and drinking at the bar. That could be you blissfully laughing and drinking . . . if you didn't have their kids.

More Ammo, Please

Sure, sometimes it's a larf to go to a cheesy themed restaurant. But annoying kids are annoying kids no matter where they are. Let's say you're at Medieval Times. Yes, there are no utensils and, yes, there is jousting by a bunch of working actors, but kids don't have to behave like dragons. Even at Medieval Times you shouldn't get hit on the head with a yam. This is why Arthur and Guineivere never had kids together.

Adrianne Frost

It's even worse if you're in a more "civilized" eatery, like Denny's or Cracker Barrel Old Country Store, because you expect a slightly higher level of decorum. When neighboring siblings decide that they're going to have a food fight, nobody asks for your permission. Mashed potatoes and mac 'n' cheese start flying like it's a Gallagher show. You can't move fast enough to cover yourself with the vinyl, checked tablecloth, and thus end up with taters in your hair.

Booths and Blinds

Booth seats are made like old car seats—springy. And kids love to bounce up and down, endangering the lives of people next to them. They turn their seating area into a jungle gym, swinging from light fixtures. If they can reach high enough, it's a hoot to pull down any dusty adjacent blinds and send blinding sunlight and dust bunnies directly into your eyes. Then, knowing they did something destructive, they hide behind the seat, popping their heads up and down, peering at you like they're in Whack-a-Mole. Oh, to have a foam mallet with which to wallop their little asses right back into the hole.

How delightful is it when kids find God. Back in the old days Sunday school was held at the same time as worship. It was a lovely segregation. Somehow that situation changed, and now kids go to regular service with their moms and dads. Nothing initiates irritability more than having to sit on hard wooden pews, listening to a sweaty guy in a robe talk about Jesus.

There are plenty of opportunities for kids to expel energy in church. Getting up for communion, a dad collars his screaming boy, insisting, "You *will* receive the body and blood of Christ, or no PlayStation!" I have seen one or two hooligans try to nip from the collection plate. Kids' choir always has at least one robed tyke who thumps the back of another's head with a hymnal. And Christmas pageants allow everyone to be a diva, even the poor kid who plays a sheep. There is no reverence from kids in church. That's why no one likes it when Other People's Kids are in their house. Not even God.

Theme Parks and Other Places You Go to Have Fun

Loverboy wrote "Everybody's Working for the Weekend," and, God love their washed-up souls, they were right. After the nine-to-five grind, we need to relax and have a good time. Nothing brings a thunderstorm to your sunny day more than Other People's Kids.

Pluto's in Grave Danger!

Most theme parks include rides and amenities that appeal to older crowds. Yet the kids still rule. The abundance of sensory overload and lack of rules in a theme park are obscene. There are no sidewalks, so kids have permission to run anywhere they want. And every three feet is a stand offering some kind of sugary treat. You may think it perverse to eat an ice-cream version of SpongeBob, but kids delight in it. Even the French fries have high-fructose corn syrup in them. By the time the clock strikes noon, the sunburned toddlers and tweens are faster, louder, and more irritable than a speed-metal band.

Even with the invention of the E-ZPass and other tricks meant to make your wait in line for rides shorter, you still have to queue up with at least a handful of these overstimulated kids. They're busy hanging off of ropes, swinging like lemurs on coke. If their parents are holding a space for them, they run freely through the maze of waiting people, bumping into and stepping on everyone's feet. Kids always delight in cutting in line, giving you a shit-eating grin, like they've achieved world domination. Other kids can end up crying and pitching a fit by sitting on the ground and refusing to move. To get the line to move faster, their moms or dads grab their arms and drag them, screaming along the concrete while they go limp, like Gandhi.

If all that weren't complicated enough, certain rides are not appropriate for certain children. For instance you wouldn't take your small child on the Incredible Hulk Coaster at Universal's Islands of Adventure; you'd take them to the Cat in the Hat ride. Yet some parents insist on bringing their kids past the YOU MUST BE THIS TALL sign. When a family gets to the front, parents hold up the line for the rest of us by inevitably and futilely arguing with the teenage ride operator that they've waited on line "for an hour," and no, they "didn't see the sign," and "C'mon!" Unfortunately, other kids are tall enough and old enough to spend the wait time jumping up and down, screeching about how excited they are. "This ride's gonna be awesome!" they yell, flopping around

Adrianne Frost

like chimps. But when they get to the front, all the color drains from their red, freckled faces. They start freaking out, right before takeoff, tugging at the straps or safety bar, begging to be immediately put on solid ground. It takes fifteen minutes to lock the gears on the ride and get the little pussies out of their harnesses and off, then another fifteen minutes to reset the ride to its specifications so you can *finally* take off.

For the high cost of admission, there should be adults-only entrances, adults-only lines, adults-only sections, and best of all, adults-only days. Disney has a wonderfully air-conditioned kennel for people's pets. Perhaps kids could be kept there as well.

Don't Leave the Light On for Them

If you can request a smoking or nonsmoking room, there really should be child-free floors offered in hotels. We'd all sleep better if kids didn't get a kick out of the funny fart noise a doorstop makes, so we don't have to hear that *thwubbbb* repeated over and over again. If there were a child-free floor, you could wake up to the sound of your alarm instead of cartoons blaring from the next room. At the very least, they could also pad the walls, so you don't have to hear the *thud thud thud* of the Daytona 500 racing up and down the hall, back and forth to the ice machine, and then hearing the sound of ice being chucked at the walls, barely missing some kid's head.

The free continental breakfast is a thoughtful gesture, but the hotel should deliver it to your door. That way, you don't have to deal with a fat, sticky hand stealing the last doughnut or kids arguing with their parents about wanting another bowl of Frosted Flakes. What starts out as a lovely breakfast area with croissants and coffee quickly turns to Hiroshima after three families swoop in for free eats.

Finding no sanctuary inside the hotel, it seems like such a tranquil idea to lounge by the pool. You envision lying out on the plastic chaise, sunglasses over your eyes, rays hitting your body. Then the first cannonball comes. If there's a lifeguard on duty, you're screwed, because the pool is then another area where kids can roam unsupervised by their parents. Free to whoop it up, they dive and splash, and then erratically struggle to get out of the water, running and slapping their wet feet on the concrete. Tiny droplets of water hit you from all directions like minitorpedoes.

Usually the depths only go to four or six feet, so kids aren't in danger of drowning, which allows them to dominate all areas of the pool. Creating deeper areas would be dangerous, so I suggest painting sharks, piranhas, and barracudas

Adrianne Frost

on a section of the pool floor to frighten them away. Hand out pamphlets entitled *Adults Only—Killer Fish Repellant* to the grown-ups. Adults would have their own section of the pool, and there'd be no tiny stragglers.

Viva Las Diapers!

Vegas! What have you done? In the early nineties, Las Vegas decided that its tourism should include kids. Enter the Excalibur hotel, Adventuredome at Circus Circus, and even roller coasters. The whole city became a kiddie pool and families jumped right in. Talk about buzz kill. Who wants to order a dominatrix up to their room after passing kids running around the Emerald City in the MGM Grand?

There is no reason for kids to be in Vegas. It's not Orlando. Vegas is for gambling, drinking, and getting married to a stripper at the Little White Wedding Chapel. Kids aren't even allowed in the casinos, but you'll see them traipsing across the slots floor with their parents or, even worse, all alone looking for their parents. It ain't Disney. It's not even a carnival at a fair ground. It's Las friggin' Vegas, a city built by mobsters and showgirls. Families should take a trip to the Grand Canyon. I mean the one that was built by nature, not the one between a hooker's legs.

Places You Go to Relax

Is any place still sacred? If you want quiet time, you're hard pressed to find it anywhere but your home. No wonder porn movie houses are doing so well; it's the only refuge we can find.

Museums

It's not funny to say *"Pee-casso"* over and over again. Well, it is a little, but not in the sanctity and quiet of a museum. Museums are essentially libraries of art. Quiet is necessary to enjoy them. The acoustics in museums are really awful. An echo is tenfold. When Other People's Kids discover the

Adrianne Frost

wonders of a museum's echo, they milk it for all it's worth. You can hear stomping, clapping, and hooting from three galleries over. And come on, do parents really think their kid understands *The Starry Night*? No, they're too busy turning Michelangelo's *David* into an excuse to laugh at a naked man's pee pee. Kids also don't understand DO NOT TOUCH, or DO NOT CROSS ROPES. To them, touching art is like playing with an Etch A Sketch—they think their grubby prints are erasable with a shake. This is why they have children's museums. Places like that are created to keep kids out of proper museums. They give kids things to do with touchy-feely interactive exhibits. Kids need a place to go where they can make their own art. Weave a potholder, Timmy; don't rain on my Monet.

Zoos

Zoos are fast changing their names to "conservation societies" in hopes that they will seem boring and children will stop going. Zoos are educational facilities. Enclosures are made to imitate the

natural habitat of the animal. Other People's Kids foul things up when they throw a straw, pennies for luck, or Doritos over the railing. These aren't pigeons; you can't just throw them something to eat. And foreign objects or food could actually kill the animal. I guess that's a small price to pay for seeing a howler monkey nosh on a waffle cone.

Zoos are also not places for kids to give a shout out to their favorite species. When a kid's banging on the glass, yelling, "Hey, monkey! Hey, monkey!" you can see the silverback gorilla staring at them, thinking, "Were it not for this triple-paned wall, I'd kick your ass, kid." Do they really believe a lion is going to look up and acknowledge them for shouting, "Roaaaar!"? Well, maybe, but only to contemplate if with a running start, it could leap over the safety moat and turn them into lunch.

In the African Savanna, kids would be the weakest,

Adrianne Frost

smallest Thomson's gazelle. They may be able to run fast, but not fast enough to survive being eaten. At zoos, what if we put kids in the exhibits, where there's a chance they'll be lunch. In the bear den, they'll have to be quiet, and in the monkey cage, they're sure to have poo flung at them. See how they like it.

Parks

You've brought a blanket, bottled water, and your favorite novel. The birds are singing. Your lover or friends are next to you. The sky is azure, no clouds in sight. You lay back in this eden to close your eyes and take a nap, and a child runs across your setup, landing his Air Jordan sneakers in your olive loaf. Thank goodness he caught that Nerf ball!

OPK turn public parks into their own backyards. They become kings or queens of the jungle by leaping on rocks, kicking up dirt, and beating their chests with Tarzan yells. KEEP OFF THE GRASS signs are of no use here. Kids crawl under or over the protective fencing to trample the seedlings or dig up divots of freshly grown grass. After their parents grill dogs and burgers on public pits, the monsters eat greedily and leave paper plates smeared with condiments all over the ground. Plastic cups with bits of soda surround the trash cans. Flies migrate from children's litter to your area.

As you sit trying to soak up some sun and fresh air, a soapy bubble pops on your head, dripping dishwashing liquid down your face. The kids have broken out the giant bubble makers. If that weren't enough, they also have Super Soaker water guns that inescapably miss the target and squirt onto your serene picnic.

Cautionary Tales:	
Movies and Television Shows that Were Made for a Reason	
Movies	**Television Shows**
The Exorcist	*Wife Swap*
Child's Play	*Take My Kids, Please*
Village of the Damned	*Growing Up Gotti*
It's Alive	*Trading Spouses*
Kindergarten Cop	*Nanny 911*
Rosemary's Baby	*The Brady Bunch*
Children of the Corn IV	*Diff'rent Strokes*

Adrianne Frost

Parents Think It's Cute but It Isn't: Baby Blogs

I long for the old days when people were ashamed of their emotions and kept their problems to themselves. It's tiring enough to hear about a baby's problems and progressions, but do we really need to read a blog that chronicles, in sickening detail, the baby's problems and progressions?

Talking relentlessly about a child is self-indulgent as it is, but to take the time to actually log on the Web and record every dump, laugh, and sleepless night? That's obsessive. Fine, people need an outlet. When I was young, we used what was called a diary (complete with padlock). As I got older the diary became a journal, and then that journal turned into therapy. Never once did I feel the need to vent about my troubled childhood for *millions to see.*

It's sad when part of being a parent's job includes blogging. Imagine if those twenty hours a week at the computer was converted into time *with* their children. Maybe then they'd find the validation they so desperately and publicly seek.

These words may look like types of furniture from IKEA, but in fact are actual noises I have heard kids make:

Barrrrr!	Nufffff!
Wahhhhhh!	Chumb!
Dooooot!	Gunahhh!
Pfffffft!	Hissssss!
Flaarhart!	Djiiit!
Zaphazat!	Farrrrrrley!

Quiz for Parents: Not *My* Baby!

Who's making all that trouble? Certainly not your baby! Are you sure? Take this eye-opening quiz to see if Other People's Kids are your own (make sure to keep track of your points for each selection you make):

1. **You're at a party, holding your baby. Suddenly, a stink rises from somewhere. Is it:**

   a. your child? (5 pts)

   b. the French onion dip? (2 pts)

   c. someone's Drakkar Noir? (1 pt)

Adrianne Frost

2. **You're enjoying pizza at Chuck E. Cheese. Twenty children emerge screaming from the ball pit, yelling "Poopy! Poopy!" What has happened?**

   a. Your child is flinging poo. (5 pts)

   b. Poopy the Puppy has just come out to greet the kids. (2 pts)

   c. Twenty children have to simultaneously make a BM. (1 pt)

3. **We are on line at the grocery store. You see me sticking my tongue out at your child. Is it because:**

   a. your child gave me the grubby finger? (5 pts)

   b. I am mentally deficient? (2 pts)

   c. I am trying to touch my nose? (1 pt)

4. **The day-care center workers are concerned about the bite marks on several children's arms. How did those bite marks appear?**

   a. Your child's teeth. (5 pts)

   b. Bats. (2 pts)

   c. Magic. (1 pt)

5. **You are testing vacuum cleaners at Sears. The sound of shattering glass is heard. Is it:**
   a. your child heaving drills at passersby? (5 pts)
   b. a terrorist attack? (2 pts)
   c. "Jesus!"? (1 pt)

6. **The fresh cookies you baked for your mother's wake are gone. Your child blames Carl. Is Carl:**
   a. your child's alter ego? (5 pts)
   b. a bandit who steals cookies, whose name your child happens to know? (2 pts)
   c. "Jesus!"? (1 pt)

7. **Back from a romantic dinner, you and your spouse come home to find the babysitter crying and the house in disarray. Who caused this?**
   a. Your children. (10 pts if you've got two kids)
   b. That crackhead babysitter. (2 pts)
   c. Wild rhinos! (I will also accept the answer "Jesus!") (1 pt)

8. **Who yelled "Noooooooooooooooooo!" when asked to quiet down at Cousin Ruth's wedding?**

Adrianne Frost

a. Your child. (5 pts)

b. Cousin Ruth. (2 pts)

c. I didn't hear anything. (1 pt)

9. **True or false: Your child just kicked me.**

    a. True. (5 pts)

    b. False. (0 pts)

10. **If your child were an animal, he/she would be:**

    a. a badger. (3 pts)

    b. a hyena. (2 pts)

    c. a kangaroo. (1 pt)

    d. all of the above. (10 pts)

Scoring

If your score is between:

40–60 points: The problem is your child. No doubt about it. He broke it, she stole it, and you ignored it.

20–40 points: You have rationalized the reasons for the incidents around you. What killed Grandma? Probably the fall.

0–20 points: I want to live in the dreamworld where you reside. A world of happiness, silence, and Jesus.

About a year ago I was dating a woman with two young children—one five-year-old girl, one four-year-old boy. It was declared at the onset of the relationship that she was a "package deal," and her kids came first. She wanted me to get to know them.

But shortly thereafter I was forbade to discipline them in any way. Now, I get how a woman may not want some random dude she happens to be dating spanking her kids (and I wasn't all that random; she and I had known each other off and on since high school), but apparently nothing that I said to them was okay either.

For example "Hey there, kid, stop jumping on my jacket" (my cell phone was in the pocket). She felt that the word kid was derogatory when referring to a four-year-old. Big fight ensues.

After the rules had been established, we were watching TV one night, and the boy decided he wanted to climb on me. Now, I also get that people who have children find this adorable. However, I do not have children.

So, since I'm not sure what I'm supposed to say or do to prevent him from climbing on me, I just let him. Now, technically he did not step on my testicle, but he stepped close enough to my testicle to illicit the male-flinch reaction. So I scoop him up, quickly but gently, and set him on the floor. He protests immediately, and she gets pissed off that I'm "not comfortable" around her kids.

I'm not sure I'd be comfortable with any human being who was allowed to step on my testicles all they wanted. — Matthew

Private Places

"NEVER RAISE YOUR HAND TO YOUR KIDS.
IT LEAVES YOUR GROIN UNPROTECTED."
—RED BUTTONS

$\mathbf{M}$y home, their parent's home, it doesn't matter. Other People's Kids become lightning bolts in a bottle when unleashed in private spaces and their parents become more permissive. Glue down your precious objects and prepare to be blinded by photo albums. Your territory becomes their territory, and their territory becomes a nightmare.

My House, My Rules

You've decided to throw a get-together to celebrate your friends and your hip and social lifestyle. You've crafted an adorable and clever Evite. You've kept an RSVP list, and bought gourmet food that costs more than the rent. The cups and plates match exactly. You've bought fresh-cut flowers, arranged perfectly. There are candles lit for ambience, and you burned a great party mix that's spinning on the CD player. It is going to be the party everyone talks about for years to come. A marvelous evening the guests will never forget. Then, just as your self-esteem is reaching its peak from the anticipated accolades, in walk friends with a party-crashing baby or toddler. Suddenly the whole event seems to melt like crayons left in the back of a car.

OPK Steal Focus

At the onset of the evening, everyone is fawning over you and your "Martha Stewart would be proud" soiree. Music is blaring, drinks are flying, . . . and in walks a family. The parents couldn't get a sitter. Or so they say. You can't help thinking it's really because they're attention-grabbing jerks, using their kid as a magnet.

The offending tot is asleep, dressed in a cashmere twin set with matching bonnet, looking as angelic as possible. Everyone starts cooing and giggling over the bundle of joy while the stuffed mushrooms and spinach-artichoke dip fall to room temperature. They marvel at the snoozing sensation, even though it doesn't do anything. Your punch bowl doesn't do zip either, but it's far less interesting. Suddenly you're back in grade school, feeling like the geeky one in the corner as the cool group fawns over the popular kid.

An hour later the child's awake and fussy, pouting and shooting tears like it needs an exorcism. Finally the crowd will back away in disgust and recognize how long you slaved over every little tiny detail of this get-together! You step up graciously to receive well-deserved compliments. But no one notices. Suddenly it's up to your guests to entertain *and* calm the tot.

Adrianne Frost

Don't Mind Me, Make a Mess!

Before your precisely planned get-together, you (and hopefully some of your better friends) cleaned the hell out of your house. You vacuumed, dusted, and mopped until pride swelled in your heart. Then your friends arrive with their kids. The kids, of course, head straight for the food, their sticky, mucky little hands getting into every dish, whether they like the fare or not. And when they taste something they don't like, they drop it wherever they please—the floor, the couch, your lap.

You may have spent hundreds of dollars to personally feed your guests. You may have spent even more to have your party catered. Wolfgang Puck could've been the chef at your party. It doesn't matter, kids don't care. They only care about what *they* want, what *they* like. And if they taste something that they find offensive to their underdeveloped palates, they don't just throw it away. They chew it up, make a face, make a sound, and spit it out onto the table. Twelve dollars per pound andouille sausage gets rolled around in a toddler's mouth, and then discharged into your hand.

When Other People's Kids get thirsty, their parents readily offer juice in a little box. This is the most ludicrous gadget ever in the history of inventions. The minute the tiny straw pops into the box, dark neon-colored liquid starts spewing onto your furniture. You're forced to follow them around neurotically, like a dog owner with a pooper-scooper, trying to ensure the virtue of your beige sofa.

Later that evening, when the families with kids are the last to leave, you make disgusting discoveries, one after the other. There are half-sucked, soggy crackers in your CD player, Juicy Juice on your DKNY throw pillows, and your condoms have all been blown up like balloons. And you'll be picking Cheerios from between the couch cushions for the next few weeks.

Now Your Pet Needs Therapy

Parents wonder why their little angel was bitten by a dog or scratched by a cat. It could have something to do with the fact that Other People's Kids think pets are toys. Just because a cat is white doesn't mean it is to be eaten like a marshmallow, sat on like a fluffy pillow, or to be colored with crayons. A cat's long tail is not meant to be yanked. It's a simple lesson: If Other People's Kids don't aggravate a cat, they won't become little, screaming scratching posts.

Adrianne Frost

Dogs are a different story. They work with a pack mentality. Some of them like to dominate. Some of them like to jump. But none of them likes to be ridden, poked, or slapped. A dog will sniff a child, lick it, circle it while sizing it up; it's instinct, not an invitation. Despite what a child may have gleaned from Scooby-Doo cartoons, not all dogs want to romp and play. How can you tell if a dog's not in the mood? If it's sleeping, eating, licking itself, or growling. That seems simple enough, right? Yet children will try to ride your Yorkie like a donkey, and end up bitten. The best thing a dog can do is hump the offending child. Then the kid'll see what it's like to be ridden by a strange creature. That'll make him think twice next time.

Censorship Begins at Home

When it comes to having Other People's Kids in your home, there's clean, and then there's clean. Not just surface clean, but "family friendly G-Rated" clean. I'm talking "the pope is coming" clean. It's exhausting. The things parents don't want their kids to see are taken to an unreasonable level. When you know kids are coming to your house, naturally, you take down the picture of Robert Mapplethorpe with a whip in his ass. Your Georgia O'Keefe framed prints may be a little too vaginal, so those get stashed in the closet. But what about the Marilyn Monroe nudes? Come on! Those are not obscene (you can barely make out her areolas!). Neither is your back massager, nor that whip from Morocco. But they have to go, just in case. You dutifully hide your art, your condoms, and Erica Jong's *Fear of Flying*. Just for fun, leave out a copy of *The Satanic Verses*.

OPK Know They're Your Guest (and Can Get Away with Murder)

Those miniature people may not know the rules of polite behavior, but they sure as hell know what they can get away with in your home. Your bookcases become jungle gyms, your Lladro figurines bounce on the floor and chip. They know that in front of your other friends, you're not going to yell or spank them. They sense you want their parents to stay. You're not going to throw anyone out. You're going to smile and say, "That's okay, my grandmother gave me that and she's dead anyway" or "Who likes priceless art? Not me!" They will take the last li'l smokey, even if they don't want it. They will jump on your bed, even if you ask them not to. They will set your rug on fire, even if there's no smoking in your house. Because they are your "guests" and because they *can*.

Parents Think It's Cute, but It Isn't: When Their Kids Have to Touch Everything

Yes, kids are curious. And there are certain textures and surfaces that invite touching (I blame *Pat the Bunny*). But it borders on compulsivity when they have to get their mitts on everything in sight. They feel the need to run their hands along metal fences, clanging as they go. They ignore the sneeze guard and put their fingers in the salad dressing and scoops of butter. They pick up dead animals and put them in their pockets, petting them like Lenny did in *Of Mice and Men*. Infants grasp long hair or dangling earrings and refuse to let go. Typically, parents make lame comments like "He's just curious" or "She's got quite a grip, doesn't she?" as your earlobes get pulled to your knees. This is why kids end up on the other side of the guardrail in zoos, protected by a female gorilla until the cops come. They just gotta touch the monkey! Well, it's not going to be so cute when the kid decides he has to handle Daddy's radial-arm saw. There's a big difference between curiosity and OCD.

OPK Make Their Parents Leave When They *Are Ready*

Later at your party things are rolling along nicely, especially because the kids are sitting in a corner with their eyelids drooping and their energy fizzled. Everyone is excited to relax, drink espresso, and nosh on butter cookies. A game of Celebrity Charades is coming as soon as you finish brewing the coffee. God*damn*, you throw a great party! As you re-enter the room, tray full of caffeinated libations, you see children, thumbs in mouths, being picked up. Great! Toss them on top of the coats in the bedroom and let's get to gab-bin'! But no, they're leaving. The *kids* are tired. Suddenly the mood shifts to neutral, and people realize how late it is as if the kids' fatigue has rubbed off on them. Thirty minutes later, you sit alone with Juan Valdez, stuffing Pepperidge Farm milanos into your mouth.

Hello, Good-bye

There's nothing worse than Other People's Kids on their own turf. It's their domain, and they guard it like an angry wombat looking for vipers. Evidence of them is everywhere, from countless photos, to laminated drawings, to fifth-place awards. The art installation in the front hallway consists of framed pictures of the kid from fetus to fifth grade, displayed

Adrianne Frost

in descending order, compulsively and perfectly arranged. Hanging next to it is a giant, gold-plated family tree, filled in completely with calligraphy that took "six months to make." Toys lie in every corner as if the kid has marked his or her territory. Crude glazed pottery figurines of green inchworms, teddy bears, and bunnies with neckties, looking like they were made in an occupational-therapy class at a rehab center, are reverently displayed on every side table. The entire house is built around the children that live there.

It's only fair to expect a certain amount of attention when you go to a friend's house. After all, *you* are the guest. Other People's Kids ruin the sacred guest-host dynamic.

The focus has shifted. No longer do your friends ask what your life is like, what you are up to, and how work is. Now, all of the attention is focused on their child. You could walk in the house with a broken arm, a parrot on your shoulder, and Johnny Depp as your date. It doesn't matter. Other People's Kids rule the roost. You are, and always will be, secondary.

Gone are the days when you went over to your friends' houses and looked at the vacation photos and videos of their trip to Hedonism II. There's no more laughing at stories of their drunken debauchery. Instead of sitting down with shared chardonnay and cigarettes, you're taken on a forty-five-minute guided tour of the new and improved childproof home. Wow, how impressive that the outlets are covered!

Do the Math: A Baby Isn't Ninety Months Old

One dog year equals seven human years. However, if your dog is, say, five, you don't say, "Scooter is thirty-five years old." Why? Because that's asinine. So, it's überannoying when parents continue to measure their kid's age in months after the first year.

You find yourself doing long-forgotten math to figure out how old the child really is. Just to make it clearer, here's a month-to-year chart (hint: round up to the nearest year):

If Mom Says:	Then:
"Jamie is fourteen months."	This kid is a year old.
"Tiffany is eighteen months."	This kid is a year and a half old.
"Matt is twenty-six months."	No, he is not—the kid's two years old.
"Katie is thirty-five months."	She's three, for God's sake.
"Thomas is sixty months."	He's too old to have his age counted in months and will have trouble getting laid in college if his parents don't stop.

OPK Suck You into Their World

You're excited to visit your friends with which you are dying to catch up. But you're not two minutes in the door before gummy child-paws tug on your fresh-pressed sleeve or pant leg. A tiny voice calls you "Aunt Whatever" or "Uncle Something" and announces they have something *very important* to show you. Hoping it's a bottle of Valium and a whiskey sour, you follow them into their room: the guest prison. This small pink or blue lair has a carousel-horse wallpaper border and shaggy train- or flower-shaped rugs. It smells of a grade-school bathroom. Trapped by the child's enthusiasm, you are forced to sit on a small, plastic chair with your ass hanging off both sides, knees up to your chin. This better be good. Hells bells, you're here to see their newest toy. Fine. You oooh and aaah and rise to leave. But wait, there's also the stuffed lobster and the new sheets

Adrianne Frost

they got and their new crayons. You become immobilized as the chair begins to crack beneath you and the kid keeps piling things onto your lap. Then, when you think the torture has stopped and you can break free of the fluffy chains, you are asked to share their art desk and do some coloring.

Once stuck in that room, you are a part of their world and bizarre games. Don't walk through the force field; be monosyllabic; the floor is on fire! You're King/Queen Doo-Doo, and you have scales. Watch out! There's a monster that likes to eat fat people! If you don't participate in these games, you're the mean adult who wouldn't play with the creative and innocent child.

Since you're playing their make-believe games, suggest one of your own. Call it Hostage, use invisible rope and duct tape to bind them to a chair, and "cover" their mouth. The goal is for the kid to remain alone in the room, as your hostage, until you come back and free them. They can try to get loose, but let them know those ropes are impenetrable and the duct tape is soundproof. If they can stay as your hostage for one hour, you will return to free them! Close the door quietly, returning to the party. Should anyone ask where the kid is, tell them, "Oh, just playing a little game."

Walking on Eggshells

Okay, the days of parties consisting of smoking weed and then eating cookie dough may have passed for most of us, but when did a party for adults (that happens to be peppered with kids) become an Orwell novel? Suddenly, you have to be careful what you bring, be careful what you say, be careful where you put things, and be careful what you set as an example. You rehearse your acceptable "fudges," "darns," and "gosh darn its." You can't forget Little Brother is watching. He stands stiffly before the television, dressed in a rigid gray uniform, watching *Dora the Explorer* with one trained eye and you with the other, ready to repeat any obscenity he hears or ask questions about any overheard risqué tale. And God forbid you're a well-endowed female. Make sure you're in a buttoned-up shirt or plated armor. Any infant who didn't have dinner will reach for your great bongos, gearing up for a prêt-à-porter meal.

Gotta Sing!

All night you've been hearing about eight-year-old Norman's prodigious rendition of "Memory." He keeps telling all of the adults that he's singing it with his class at the next assembly. You endure stories of how he's practiced at home all week and how his voice is a gift from God. You can't get away from the subject. Finally after dinner, dessert, and drinks, Norman squirms his way up to the front of the room, ever so reluctantly. His mom hits play on the tape recorder, and everyone in the room sits uncomfortably through the taped intro of his teacher on the piano. He begins singing. The notes are as sour as a lemon fresh from the tree. They assault your senses so much that you have to sit on your hands to keep from covering your ears. You bite the insides of your cheeks so you don't laugh at the poor bugger. His little arms repeat rehearsed gestures that coincide with every word. And it's funny that the song is "Memory," because he can't remember some of the lyrics. Somewhere Andrew Lloyd Weber has dug a grave, just so he can spin in it. When it's over, everyone claps as if they've just seen a crippled street mime, except for Mom and Dad, who stand and cheer like the ardent fans they are.

Parents Think It's Cute, but It Isn't: Putting Their Child's Picture on Everything

With the invention of modge podge and the popularity of crafting, utilizing kids' photos has reached far beyond the standard photo album. In the last few years scrapbooking has become a phenomenon. Brads, acid-free pens, photo corners, ink pads and stamps . . . the sales are through the roof. It's gone perversely further, though, with the introduction of personalized everyday objects. I'm talking photo-printed tote bags, tissue-box covers, coasters, commemorative plates, mugs, aprons, T-shirts, and vases. Even worse is receiving these items as gifts. You then have to display them in your home and look like *you're* the obsessed relative/friend. I think they should go all out if they want to put their kid's sticky, smiling face on everything. Who wouldn't cherish a unique and distinctive cigarette lighter, tampon holder, condom wrapper, or bong?

OPK Get to Stay Up Late When There's Company

When you attend a party at your friend's house, you expect a relaxing and fun evening where you aren't worried about things going smoothly. If people bring their kids, mess up the house, and leave early, you won't be bothered. After all you are a guest, not a host, and should be able to kick back and nosh on a veggie platter or pig in a blanket with no concerns.

But Other People's Kids poop on a party no matter whose house it is. They get very excited when guests are in

Adrianne Frost

their house, allowing few moments of silence or enjoyment. They expel their energy early in the evening, busily showing off new toys and new tricks, and playing incessantly. As the night marches onward, they get increasingly tired and cranky. Nonetheless, if the party's going strong, they get to stay up. There's no use putting them to bed—the noise will keep them awake. So, they continue to stay up and park themselves in the fetal position on Mommy's lap, dressed in their pajamas with their thumb in their mouth. But fifteen minutes into sitting quietly and comfortably in that spot, they begin to whine.

"I want a drink and chips and cookies," they say, interrupting Mommy's conversation about Susan Sontag and looking at you like you don't matter.

"Not right now," says Mommy, trying to continue her chat.

"*What* not right now?" interrupts the kid again.

"You can't have that right now," she replies as calmly as possible.

"What not right now?" repeats the youngster, teasing the mother. "The drink, the chips, or the cookies?"

The room has become increasingly uncomfortable. Everyone wants this kid to go. Daddy picks up the kid with a loud "Oooookay." Fun's over. It's bedtime for Bozo. The kid is exhausted, but doesn't want to go, so begins the screaming and crying all the way down the hall. Yup, fun's over for everyone. The jovial mood of the party has just gone down the toilet.

When Other People's Kids finally go to bed, the whole atmosphere of the party changes. First, you're all incredibly uncomfortable after the hissy fit you just witnessed. Second, everyone has to whisper, terrorified of waking up the child. Party games are a no go—no more Outburst, Yahtzee, or Twister, unless you want to play like Marcel Marceau. The music is switched from Led Zeppelin to Tori Amos, and people begin telling stories of their abused childhoods. The candles are extinguished, and the night is over.

Babysitting . . . or DEATH BY HAM?

I performed an unscientific, nonexistent study to determine which people would prefer: helping out with Other People's Kids, or being beaten to death with a ham. In conclusion, with the exception of babysitting, most individuals would rather be beaten to death with a ham than take care of Other People's Kids.

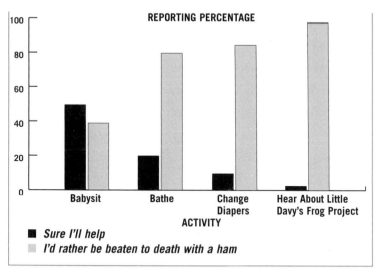

REPORTING PERCENTAGE

Activity axis labels: Babysit, Bathe, Change Diapers, Hear About Little Davy's Frog Project

ACTIVITY

■ *Sure I'll help*
▨ *I'd rather be beaten to death with a ham*

This Is When She Crowned

Once that baby pops out, all bets are off. The new parents—your formerly fun-loving, freewheeling friends—are no longer humans. They're babyoids, adults ruled and regulated by their babies. It's bewildering and unsettling. All conversations and correspondence revolve around the children—from what the kids do, to how long it took them to come into the world. The mothers' bodies become part of Ripley's Believe It or Not! museums, performing unheard of feats. Never has the phrase "too much information" been more appropriate, and never have you felt more obsolete.

Have You Met My Vagina?

When you first became acquainted with your dear friend, or your dear friend's wife, you never expected to also become friends with her genitalia. I mean, there's close, and then there's *close*. All of a sudden, because she's gone through the miracle of birth, she's willing to show all—and I mean all— by sharing the delivery video. The pressure to view this D-grade porno is intense because the couple insists you watch it. You don't want to see it. You don't need to see the birthing tape. You don't want to see the birthing tape. Your dog had puppies once and that was enough. You'll never eat tacos again.

The Story of Her Labor

Dear Friend,
Last week when we got together for lunch, you opened our conversation by saying, "I realize the story of my labor is much more interesting for me

than for you, but . . ." Stop right there. You're right. It is more interesting for you than for me, because it was your delivery. If I don't ask you about it, don't tell me. I understand that seeing your own blood was disconcerting and that it was everywhere, but don't relay that tidbit when I'm pouring vinaigrette on my salad. Then they said you couldn't deliver vaginally? I won't be ordering my steak rare. You saw the placenta perched on your stomach? I just lost my appetite. You used a midwife? I don't even know what that is. Over dessert and coffee, I don't want to hear about the epidural, how many centimeters you were dilated, how long the ordeal took, and what you did with the afterbirth. I get it—your vagina works. When you are ready to have an adult conversation that does not include Lamaze, call me.

Love,

Your friend

Feel the Kick

Almost as creepy as watching the birth of a baby is actually feeling the baby when it's still in the belly. It's weird. It's John Hurt in *Alien*. No one normally makes a habit out of touching their friend's bellies, so why should it be any different if it's distended? Often you're not even asked, they just grab your hand and stick it forcefully on their stomach, just over the area that was formerly their belly button and is now the thermometer that pops out on the Thanksgiving turkey. When you're at a Mexican restaurant, after eating the number eight combo platter, and the gas bubbles start popping around, you don't grab someone's hand, press it onto your tummy, and say, proudly, "That must be the cheese!"

My Feet Are So Swollen

Pregnant women's ailments are hard for me to relate to. Unless they're talking about aching tootsies from perusing the sales at Macy's, those preggos can bitch somewhere else. Pregnant women chose this path of weight gain and waddling. Pregnant women need to own up to the fact that they unlocked the chastity belt, forgot their Pill, or used a ten-year-old condom before they start droning on about the perils of pregnancy. Suck it up, buttercup. You kneaded the dough that put that bun in the oven. There should be a group, like AA, where pregnant women get together and bitch. Then you don't have to hear it every time you call your expecting buddies.

Adrianne Frost

The Twelve Steps of Pregnant Complainers

We:

1. admitted that we were powerless over bitching about our pregnancies, that our lives had become unmanageable.

2. came to believe that a cookie or some other chock-full-of-chocolate treat could restore us to sanity.

3. made a decision to stop complaining to our nonpregnant friends.

4. made a commitment to call our PC sponsor only when we feel cranky, swollen, or farty.

5. apologized to our nonpregnant friends for all of the times we sucked out of their lives by droning on about our stretch marks and dry nipples.

6. were sort of ready to remove all these defects of character.

7. humbly tried to remove our shortcomings.

8. made a list of all persons we had bored to tears with our bitching, and became willing to make amends with them all.

9. made direct amends to such people wherever possible, even if it meant flying cross-country.

10. continued to take personal inventory, and when we felt the urge to overflow with grumbling about our pregnancy, promptly left the room.

11. became a binge eater, learning to stuff our feelings, and leave our childless friends alone, whenever a meeting was not possible.

12. having had a spiritual awakening as the result of these steps, we tried to carry this message to Pregnant Complainers everywhere, and to practice these principles in all our affairs until the baby is born.

Baby Pictures

"Look at him! Will you just look at him? There he is!" Well, I hate to say it, but he looks just like every other magenta, slimy, pink baby, fresh out of the womb. Until they get to a certain age, all newborns are erasers with hats. And fifty out of fifty-five pictures are of the kid sleeping. I'm bored already. If we're going to be forced to view Other People's Kids' baby pictures, make the photos more interesting. C'mon, you're creative. I saw the World's Greatest Grandpa T-shirt you decoupaged.

Parents should Photoshop the nine hundred pictures of the baby sleeping into international locals: "Here's Henry sleeping on Stonehenge, here's Henry sleeping up the side of the Eiffel Tower, here's Henry sleeping with Lenin. Oh, and here's Henry sucking on Eleanor Roosevelt's tit!"

Adrianne Frost

Elaborate Birthday Parties for Infants and Toddlers

A lovely and ornate invitation arrives in the mail. Embossed and sealed with a wax initial, it is the pinnacle of taste. Is one of your friends getting married? Have you been invited to a royal wedding? Opening it with anticipation and reverence, you find an engraved picture of Barney on the cover and the request of your presence at Cindy's second birthday extravaganza.

When parents throw obscenely ornate parties for their toddlers, it's more for themselves than for their kids. Babies don't know the difference between having a highly crafted birthday party at a sophisticated restaurant and having a pared-down celebration in a concrete storage rental unit. As long as there's cake and balloons, they don't care and won't remember it anyway. The kid falls asleep before the halfway point. What's even worse is when the party is at a "restaurant," like McDonald's. You're not even going to get fancy eatin's or cheap booze. Sure, the food is gratis and that's always a plus, but the money spent on the gift ordered from the baby gift registry cancels out any freebies that you scarf down.

As each of the millions of presents are violently ripped open by the baby, the gift giver is thanked by Mommy or

Daddy as the object is passed around for inspection. Do the masses approve of the dowry? Will you be invited to the next useless soiree? Meanwhile the child is already whizzing through the paper on the next box, because that's all she cares about: the wrapping paper! This ridiculous party could be about nothing but wrapping paper and the kid would be happy.

All of this commotion and activity is for a two-year-old, who isn't quite sure what the fuss is all about, but who will dance up a storm when their parents push play on the boombox and "Who Let the Dogs Out" fills the room. She'll shimmy and shake for the attention, as a circle of adults clap and giggle. You're busy checking your watch or e-mailing on your Blackberry, counting down the minutes until you can escape. It's easy to slip away unnoticed once the crappy clown or magician arrives.

You're Not Grandma

You don't want to talk to Other People's Kids on the phone. You don't want to talk to your friends while they are dealing with their kids. When you call your friend's house, you wish to talk to her on the phone. You don't say, "Hey, is Harry Jr. there? I'd like to hear him gurgle." So much time is wasted as the kid tries to form words and sentences with a parent coaching them in the background. You rarely talk to your mother when she calls, and for the same reasons.

If you call your friends or they call you, nothing is more annoying than hearing them scold, applaud, or fuss with their children. It's the ultimate distraction, because they can't just mute or turn off the kid. I've asked. They're preoccupied with making lunches or tying shoelaces among the screaming, with the phone cradled in the crook of their neck. You try to get the message through that they can call you back, preferably when the kids are in college, but they can't hear you. Grandma may delight in hearing a parent fuss with their kids, but you're hanging up after three minutes.

Parents Think It's Cute, but It Isn't: Putting Their Child on the Answering Machine

Beginning in the 1970s answering machines entered most homes. Inevitably joke messages began popping up on outgoing tapes everywhere. Cassettes of song parodies, humorous impersonations, and political wit sold in stores and on television. An invention that was meant to streamline the world's time management turned into a show-case for pranksters and amateur comedians. Instead of a few words and a beep, we had to sit through a side-splitting monologue for three minutes.

Now that people create personalized answering-machine messages, more time is exhausted with the needless use of putting their child on the outgoing message. Instead of the drawn-out game of yester-day, the message begins with the typical "Hi, this is _____ (Mom) and _____ (Dad) and . . ." Silence. Giggles. Then: "C'mon, Harry Jr. Say 'and Harry Jr.!'" Giggles. By this time the person on the other end is frustrated and bored. Giggles and more giggles as the caller impatiently rolls their eyes. Finally Harry Jr. manages something to the tune of "Harp-gah." *Then* comes the beep. If you haven't slammed the phone down by this time, you've completely forgotten why you called in the first place.

Guess What (Insert Name) Did?

Unless it's cured cancer, who gives a shit? Not everything is a miracle. We all learned to walk, talk, read, and write at about the same age. Nobody anointed our feet for that.

Adrianne Frost

Nonetheless, friends regale us with the most inane events: Timmy drew a bunny, Rachel got potty trained, Josie learned to ride a bike. Here are things that would impress me: Hallie saved a drowning calf, Roger foretold a fire, Charlie got stigmata. I doubt if Mary bragged about Jesus's first baby tooth. I'm far more apt to listen and care if it's an accomplishment that will nominate the kid for sainthood.

Sweet Nothings

It's one thing to have your friend use baby talk around her kid. It's quite another to have her use it with you, at brunch . . . no kids in sight. The kind of sibilant speak that pours forth to a child is fine. They need things simplified. But it's just embarrassing for a grown person to tell a waiter she'll have a "gin on da wocks," and then apologize to you for the slip. The errors continue with everything from "Excuse me while I use the potty" to "Oooh, someone needs a nap!" when you complain about work. It's a shock that she doesn't cut your meat for you. They keep saying how sorry they are; they're in baby mode. Really? If they're truly sorry, why don't they friggin' stop, then? Otherwise no brunch with you until the kid's eighteen.

Scooby-Doo and Innuendo

Some parents shield their children from everything because they're afraid of bad influences. Expletives aren't just mouthed, spelled out, or whispered, they're banned. You can't even say a word that *sounds* like a curse word. They aren't allowed to see movies with guns (not even *Toy Story*), or "politically incorrect" flicks (see Mammy in *Gone with the Wind*). Yet they watch *CSI* in full view of their children. *Certainly* a seven-year-old can gather some educational value from a dead whore's autopsy. What they don't realize is that these kids, so sheltered from all outside sources, will end up rebelling and getting into even more trouble than they ever thought possible. They'll end up pregnant and riding the dragon. Do they really believe that Rapunzel remained pure after being sequestered that whole time? Hell no, she was banging every knight in the kingdom and drinking mead until all hours five minutes after she shimmied down that tower. Anyone who's ever heard of an Amish Rumspringer knows the perils of locking up a teen for too long.

Adrianne Frost

How to Deal

"'CUTE' . . . 'CUTE' . . . THAT WORD USED TO MEAN SOMETHING."
—RAY ROMANO

O kay, finally, here's a place where you can blow off steam. After suffering through the indignities brought on by children and their parents, it's time to exact your revenge.

Turning the Tables

1. On Kids

There are lots of ways to get out your ya ya's without seriously hurting anyone. Besides, kids don't consider *your* feelings when they're blowing out your eardrums, lofting dumplings at you in Denny's, or peeing on your leg, so screw 'em. Remember that when you're afraid to teach those miniature morons a lesson.

Behold the foil-proof tactics (and use them wisely):

- **Boo!:** Perfecting a scary, dead-on stare is a great way to make kids crap their pants, especially when they're laughing it up and running about willy-nilly. If a couple of kids are darting around store racks, chasing and hooting and hollering, don't look at them and say, "Excuse me" incredulously. Just stare. Glare and stare, that's my tactic. Pretend you're in a war zone and they're privates goofing off. Look at them like you really don't think anything they do is amusing, like you're one of those people their mothers warned them about. As far as they know you have a burlap sack and a big van waiting downstairs to take them away to sweatshop slavery. Don't avert your gaze until they back away slowly, and then cheerily go back to shopping.

- **Join In:** If you've got an Artist Formerly Known as Kid on your hands, or a fit-throwing diva squirming and seizuring on the floor, don't stare or run away, join in on the fun. If they're banging on the cart and singing, stand next to them shaking a cup full of change yourself. As much as possible, stay in rhythm to their wonky beat. Start to sing at the top of your lungs. Just croon gibberish and make up your own tune; throw in a couple of audible curse words for them to learn just for fun. Should the crib lizard be pitching a hissy fit on the ground, lay down next to them and start jerking and screaming. Speak in tongues ("Mondila, Tuesdila, Wednesdila") or whine about something you can't have ("I want my youth back!"). It's up to you whether to add dribbling. I guarantee they'll be so confused, they'll stop what they're doing. Although you may end up with someone trying to help you to not swallow your tongue, it's worth it.

- **Ain't That a Shame:** Carry a picture in your wallet of one of those underprivileged kids from TV. When you see a child begging for a toy or money or candy, pull it out and show it to them. Tell them that Ognatu never gets what *he* wants, not even food. Let them know that Ognatu works in a factory that has no windows or bathroom, and he made that toy for money or candy but never gets to enjoy the spoils of his labor. Tell them that if they don't stop, they will be sent to live with Ognatu and work beside him in the factory that has no windows or bathroom. To top it all off explain that Ognatu used to be a little, happy, American child just like them, named Timmy, who whined when he didn't get what he wanted. Stare at the child for a good three seconds in silence. Put the photo back in your wallet and walk away quietly.

- **Calling Their Bluff:** A lot of kids think handicapped people are funny. Why? Kids are inconsiderate idiots, that's why. The next time some kid starts pretending to be retarded as his friends laugh, go up to him and talk to him like he *is* retarded. Then laugh with his friends at him. Say things like, "Aren't retards funny?" Point a lot.

- **Nip It in the Bud:** When someone's child starts bragging about all the toys they have, ask them if they can play with all of them at once. If they say no, then what's the use in telling you that? Unless they were bragging. They weren't bragging, were they? Because if they were bragging, that would make them real little shits, wouldn't it? And they know what happens to little boys and girls who brag too much, don't they? They have all their possessions taken away and given to children who don't brag. Like Ognatu.

- **Quietly Warn Them:** Out of earshot of their folks, beckon them to you and let them know there are consequences for their behavior. It's usually a good bet to tell them that the following people will become very, very sick if they don't shape up: the Easter Bunny, Santa Claus, the Tooth Fairy, and Grandma. Or let them know that you can send them back to their alien planet or their real parents. Say it with a smile.

- **Prove Them Wrong:** So, Smarty McSmartpants is bragging about the planets she learned in science class. The worst part is that she knows things you never bothered to learn. Even though you're an intelligent, successful adult, you feel foolish. Tell her she's mistaken. Make up facts. Ask her to tell you about the planet Jupitune. She will undoubtedly deny its existence. Press on. Give details. Let her know that her teacher and parents are crazy. When her parents approach you and confront you, slowly explain that you asked about Jupiter and Neptune and have they had her checked for a developmental disorder?

- **Read to Them:** Start with *Lord of the Flies*, *Charlie and the Chocolate Factory*, or *Oliver Twist*. They'll get the message.

- **Gently Trip 'Em:** This is a last resort. This is when you've been bumped a million times or the noise is just too much and you don't feel like being particularly clever. Use just the tip of your foot so there's more of a stumble than a fall. Without their parents seeing, of course. When the kid points to you, raise your hands in disbelief. Smile sweetly and chuckle. Ah, kids! Who're the parents going to doubt? Not you. Why would you trip a kid? Then giggle softly to yourself and your friends.

2. On Parents

It's tiring to hear the same story about Other People's Kids' participation in the holiday pageant, and it's even harder to have to watch the video, unsolicited, five times in a row. Why can't parents just talk about politics, pop culture, or religion like the rest of us? Because they've been baby-brainwashed. Perhaps these tactics will help them understand what zombies they've turned into:

- **Force the Issue:** Laminate your pap smear and put it on the fridge. Proudly show it off the next time they come over. Pop in the video of you passing that stubborn kidney stone. Show off the memory box you created of the event!

Craft Project: Create Your Own
Commemorative Ailment Memory Box!

Why should parents have all of the crafting fun? Be proud of the drama you endured! Share your journey through the art of paper and glue.

Crafting time: 20 minutes

Skill Level: Novice

Supplies: Shadow box

     Black construction paper

     Souvenirs from your experience (photos

---

of your exams, hospital bracelet, kidney stone, pap smear, polyp, etc.) Illustrated diagrams of your anatomy, including maps of how lump, goiter, gallstone, or smear was taken printed caption(s) (suggestions: "Ow!," "Youch!" or "That's how it goes!")
Glue
Scissors
Cord for hanging

1. Remove backing of shadow box.
2. Glue black construction paper to backing and paste body diagram at an angle.
3. Attach very special souvenir to backing.
4. Glue caption(s) above souvenir.
5. Trim backing and reattach to shadow box.
6. Hang proudly with cord.

- **Obsess:** Talk incessantly about your pet's behaviors. Don't forget to repeat the same facts over and over again (catching Frisbees with precision, how often they sleep, what celebrity they look like). Go on slowly and accurately about its obsession with wadded-up paper. Get exact measurements of its bowel movements, so you can describe them in detail. Talk about the wadded-paper thing some more, seeming amazed. Ask things like, "Did I tell you about Fluffy's obsession with wadded-up paper?"

- **Fight Back:** At their house, stick your hands in the pâté, and then touch everything. Pick up the Lladro figurines with gummy paws, and then pretend to almost drop them. (Be careful not to actually drop them, you may then have to pay . . . oh wait, did they reimburse you for your decorative plate that Junior smashed? Aw, hell, go ahead and drop the bugger!) Don't apologize for anything reckless you may do.

- **Be Proud:** You bought a pair of Prada loafers at an 80 percent discount! Take photographs of them: on your feet, in the box, with the salesperson, on the bed, under good lighting. Create a photo album and force people to share it with you.

- **Get Technical:** Take your date into the bathroom with you, and then talk really loudly about his/her technique.

Adrianne Frost

Shout out each step of the urinating process and commend them for hitting the bowl. Exit the lavatory beaming with pride. Declare loudly, "Guess who made a boom-boom?"

- **Surprise Them:** You've been invited to the umpteenth baby shower, and you really don't want to go. But the guilt and pressure are killing you. To compensate for being the only childless attendee, show up at the event with something that's equally as out of place as you are: a stripper, an ounce of cocaine, a bottle of RUD-40. Maybe they'll finally get how uncomfortable you feel at those things.

- **Whistle While You Work:** It's not fair play when a coworker with kids gets to knock off early to tend to her critters while you stay late. The next time you (child-free) get asked to cover for a colleague (child-full), politely back out on account of the volunteering you do with blind, schizophrenic, homeless people. Then go play extreme Frisbee with your buddies in the park.

- **It's My Party:** Get flyers and invites printed up, summoning your friends with children to your dog's birthday celebration. Create a wish list of gifts for him. Get favors, a cake, little doggy treats, and cone-shaped hats that you force everyone to wear. Talk about how much you love your dog, and he deserves this party and you're broke; then ask your friends to chip in. Open the presents yourself and cry when you see the gifts. Lift your dog's paw and shake it, use baby speak, saying things like, "Muffin thanks you!" If you don't have a pet, celebrate Arbor Day! Tell everyone that your ancestors were Andalusian tree people.

Epilogue

Now that we've come to the end of our journey, what have we learned? Well, there's a lot more to hate than we thought, huh? When it's all put together in one place, it seems almost unbearable. It's not unbearable, not if you just let the hate flow freely like a angrily shaken sippy cup.

Feel better knowing you now have the liberty to hate Other People's Kids in the open. There's no secret club; there are plenty of us out there. You will find us rolling our eyes at a child who repeatedly throws its bottle to the ground. We are in the supermarket, staring down a crying toddler who wants ice cream. I am on the train pumping up the volume on my iPod as a little girl screeches at the top of her tiny lungs. Just throw me a glance and grit your teeth. That's all the solidarity we need.

Good luck and Godspeed.

About the Author

Jordan Matter

Adrianne Frost is an actor and comedian living in New York City. She is a panelist on VH-1's *Best Week Ever*. Adrianne has appeared on *The Daily Show* as a correspondent, *Late Night with Conan O'Brien*, *Law & Order*, *Law & Order: SVU*, and *Law & Order: Criminal Intent*. Her comic prose, "Easter Is Cancelled," was published in the 2005 edition of *The Signet Book of American Humor*.